Voices from the Graves Still follow Me

Betty Spaltenspurger

8-1-09

Voices from the Graves

Still follow Me

by
Betty Spaltensperger

Heatherwood Publishing

Elmira, Michigan

Voices from the Graves

Heatherwood Publishing
Elmira, Michigan

ISBN-10: 0-9819728-5-3
ISBN-13: 978-0-9819728-5-5

Book design by: Progressive Book Marketing, LLC
Layout by: ChronosPro Publishing

Cover design by: ChronosPro Publishing

Dedication

This book is dedicated to my mother, Elisabeth Knoebl Stefan, born November 12, 1912, whose greatest dream, "to let our story be known" so that the atrocities and sufferings which happened in Yugoslavia in 1945-1947 would be known by the rest of the world.

to ....

my father, Heinrich Stefan, born July 28, 1907, whose faith and trust in God gave him the courage to find a way of escape to freedom for his family.

to ....

my three precious grandchildren Lisa Jane, Anna Kathryn, and Jacob

In Loving Memory Of

My Grandparents:
"Binder" Opa and Oma
Stefan, Johann & Rosalia/nee Hermann

My Great Grandma: Urendl
Knoebl, Regina/nee Paitz

My aunt:
Regin bas
Knoebl, Regina/nee Ebli

Relatives, friends, neighbors, and all the innocent
men, women, children, and babies who suffered and
succumbed to the horrible conditions of the Communist
concentration camps, simply because they were born of
German ancestors.

Acknowledgments

I am grateful to all who encouraged me to write and all who helped me in various ways through the years to get my memoirs published, finally making this book a reality.

To: Duane and Betty Heffner, Ed and Renee Wohlfeil, Richard and Marsha Carlson, Catherine Laurence, Kody Bigelow, Kelly Mang, Kelly Parker, Kyle Johnson, Jody Chambers, Laura Wohlfeil, Lynda Robinson, Nancy Mickey, Annick-Hivert Carthew, Howard and Sue Payne, Cindy Point, Katharina (Kathie) Schwager/nee Hercher, Rose Wright/nee Hercher, Therese Hercher, Hans Kopp, Sharon Baker.

A special thank you! to my very dear friend, "Marginchen" – Maria Regina Struck /nee Hercher. "Marginchen" spent countless hours helping me to write my memoirs. She even took vacation time to come "Up North." Her constant notes of encouragement, via the "Pony Express," kept me writing, when often I thought of just "throwing in the towel."

Special thank you! to: Kathy Quandt for coming to my rescue many times when I encountered computer problems.

With deepest appreciation to all.

Thank you Steve Smith Chronos Pro Publishing for his vision on my book cover and layout work.

A very special "Thank You!" to Denise Glesser, of Progressive Book Marketing, who did everything in her power to get my memoirs published.

THANK YOU!

Table of Contents

Preface
Earliest Childhood Recollections

It was a beautiful sunny morning in June of 1943. I had just finished my bowl of cream of wheat and intended to go outside to watch my father at work making wine barrels. I called him Dati. It was fascinating to watch him position the narrow pieces of wood side by side inside the two metal hoops and the bottom of the barrel. It was tricky to keep all those planks from collapsing. Then two other hoops were positioned near and around the top of the barrel. Of course, the wood had to be soaked in order to bend into shape. "Sim-sala-bim!" the barrel was finished. It was amazing at the speed and skill with which he worked. Everything fit perfectly. He then filled the barrel with water to check for leaks. I could watch him for hours.

Just then Mami interrupted my thought and announced that she was going to our vineyard to tie up the grape vines – that meant I was going along. I needed to tell Dati where we were going. His shop was located right next to our summer kitchen.

As I stepped outside the kitchen door, I spotted Dati bent over a barrel, tapping the hammer gently at a narrow plank of wood to align it in its place. This was Dati's busiest season. He was the only barrel maker in Sentiwan (short for our town, Batschsentiwan) who used electric machinery for making wine barrels.

Dati used to work with his father making the barrels by hand, the old fashioned way; but that involved a lot of hard work and long hours. Dati's dream was to someday have a business of his own using electric machinery. His father, "Binder" Opa (nickname- family name was Stefan) was against electric machinery and could NOT be persuaded to modernize. Therefore, Dati decided to go into business on his own.

When Knoebl Opa (Mami's father) heard about Dati's dream and his dilemma with his father's refusal to buy electric machines, he came to Dati with a proposition and said, "Henrich, we have lots of room in our yard to build a work shop. If you all move in with us, you can add on to the house and build yourself a workshop next to the wagon port.

We will lay a brick driveway wide enough so that customers can drive into our yard with their wagons to pick up their barrels. We will build two brick pillars to secure a wide wooden gate that can be locked.

The yard is big enough to store all the oak lumber you need so that you will have everything on hand. We will have electricity strung into our yard for your machines and also for the rest of the house."

After Dati listened to Knoebl Opa's suggestion, he was overjoyed and told Mami all that her father had said. They discussed the matter and decided to accept his offer. Dati got busy hiring all the necessary laborers to get the project completed.

In 1939, when I was one year old, our family (Dati, Mami, my brother, Joschi and I) moved from my "Binder" grandparents' house to my Knoebl grandparents' house.

Dati got himself a business partner, Tettman Stefan Vetter, a short, slender and witty man who was ready to pull a prank on anyone, any time. I liked him.

They bought all the electric machinery they needed; and right off, they had a booming business.

In fact, when "Binder" Opa found out how easy it was to produce the barrels, he used to come over, bring his wood, and use Dati's electric machines to make headway in his own business. I believe he was sorry that he did not give his OK when they worked together.

Grape harvest was in late September to early October and that was not far away. New barrels were in great demand. They also turned half barrels into gear-driven washing machines and made all sorts of vats and wooden tubs of various sizes.

I was all excited that we were going to the vineyard. It was a fun place to go. I was so happy that I skipped over to where Dati was working. When he saw me coming, he stopped for a moment to listen to what I had to tell him and then I announced, "We're going to the vineyard to tie up the grape vines!"

Then I planted a kiss on his cheek and skipped past the stacks upon stacks of oak wood piled up in our yard and I passed the already finished barrels lined up near our front gate that were ready to be picked up by his customers. When I reached the front gate, I waited for Mami who was already coming with her shears and raffia and a basket with our lunch.

On our way, we stopped at "Binder" Opa and Oma's house to see, if perhaps, my cousins, Schneider Lisi and Franzi would like to join us. Their mother, Rosl Bas, (Bas-meaning aunt) is my dad's youngest sister. They lived in Opa and Oma's house. "Binder" Opa's family name was actually "Stefan," Johan and Rosalia, not "Binder". However, there were so many families in our town with the surname of Stefan that it was hard to tell who was who. Therefore, each family was given a nickname by the folks of the town, a name which usually pertained to what the father's trade happened to be. For instance, Binder was a barrel maker, Bauer, a farmer, Schuster, a shoemaker, Sodash – a producer of sparkling water, etc. No one used their family name of Stefan except on legal papers.

As we entered "Binder" Opa's yard, I saw Oma smelling the roses that Dati had planted all along the fence when we lived with them. I ran over to her and greeted her with a hug and said, "We're going to the vineyard and we came to see, if perhaps, Lisi and Franzi want to come along with us." We saw each other and played together a lot. It seemed like we were always together. Lisi is one year and a half older than I and Franzi slightly a little younger. They came running out the house and agreed to join us; and away we went. It was about a half hours walk down the street called Razengasse till we came to the end and then we turned to the right. There was our vineyard.

Everyone in town owned a vineyard and each owner made his own wine. The vineyards surrounded the outskirts of Sentiwan. As far as the eyes could see, there were rows upon rows of grape vines. Our vineyard was a corner lot with 42 rows of grape vines – each row was 400 yards long.

One row was planted strictly with grafted grapes where each vine had been planted by a wooden post. The other rows were a shorter grape variety which didn't need staking. But all new shoots of the vines needed to be tied, either to a post or to each other to keep them from sprawling into the walk way.

Mami had a big job ahead of her. We helped weed between the rows which were spaced about a yard wide. We did not want weeds to interfere with the growth of the grapes; because we hoped to harvest big clusters of juicy grapes for eating. My two favorite grafted grapes were the sweet light green oblong ones and the big round black ones which we called "Ox Eyes." One grape alone was a mouth full. When we bit down on one, the juice squished out the side of our mouth. Those were delicious. When we arrived, Mami wasted no time tying up the vines using the raffia; while we three just ran up and down the rows playing hide and seek for a while before we helped weed.

We were all busy doing our chores when suddenly a strange sound in the distance broke the silence. A droning sound in the sky was coming nearer. Mami suddenly rose up and yelled, "Hurry, lie down next to the grape vines; a bomber is coming!" Fear raced through our bodies, and hurriedly, we all fell down, our faces to the ground with hands over our heads. No sooner done, when a huge bomber passed on, high, overhead. My heart was pounding and so did everyone else's I'm sure. We were so relieved when the droning sound faded into the distance. When we stood up and brushed us off, Mami admonished us that whenever we heard that sound, no matter where we were, to run for cover immediately. She did not need to say that twice – that sound put fear into our hearts.

We resumed our work; and it soon was time for a lunch break. We went to our neighbor's vineyard to wash our hands and to fetch drinking water. That vineyard used to belong to my Paitz Urendl (Great Grandpa Paitz) before he died. He had dug a well when he first planted his vineyard; and it was ours to use whenever we needed water. The "water rights" were stated in his Will. Mami had brought fresh baked bread and fried bacon for our lunch. It tasted good. All that weeding made us hungry. Lunch finished, it was back to work again.

We needed to be back home by 4:00 p.m. But this time we did not take weeding too seriously. Now each of us children did his own thing which we thought fun. My mind was now on finding a little green frog to take home as a pet. I started to look thoroughly for little tree frogs that have tiny suction cups on their feet and can cling to anything, even upside down. I wanted to take one home and put it in a jar with a stick and watch it climb up the stick and then hang upside down on the lid of the jar. I thought it fascinating. I was so preoccupied with finding a frog that time passed quickly without success. I was disappointed. I had no frog to take home. The day was spent and it was time for us to head for home.

Mami yelled out, "It's time to go! Get ready!" With face down, I drudgingly walked toward where Mami stood waiting for us to come to her. All of a sudden I saw something move; and sure enough, it was a little frog. My face lit up with glee and a big smile spanned from ear to ear. I bent down and gently put it in the palm of my hand and placed the other hand over it to keep it safe. Mami yelled, "Come on, come on, quit dawdling. We have to go!"

We were singing songs on the way back and it seemed we reached Oma's place in no time and dropped off my cousins. Then on we went to our home at the Knoebl's house.

Bringing the little frog home in the palm of my hand was a challenge. It tried to get free. Every time it wiggled, I would cup my hands a little tighter to make sure it couldn't get away. When we reached home, I couldn't wait to show Dati what I had in my hand; and when I opened my hand, to my surprise, I had a lifeless little creature, all squished. This brought tears to mine eyes; and I told myself to be more careful, next time.

As the months passed by, more and more bombers were seen flying high over Sentiwan which made us dash into our cellars for cover. However, none ever came low or dropped bombs on us. We were thankful for that.

The winter months were sad ones for me. Knoebl Oma was very sick. She had been diagnosed with liver cancer. Before she got sick, I used to pop into her room every day. Her room was located right next to our bedroom. All I had to do was step outside our room, walk a few steps down the corridor outside until I reached her door, then knock on the door and walk right in. I mostly found her standing in front of her kitchen cupboard putting a dishcloth onto something in the cupboard.

She loved to read books of romances but did not want to be seen reading during the day when she should have been busy doing her housework. Therefore, whenever she heard a person walking down the corridor coming nearer while she was reading, she would put the book into the cupboard and cover it up with a dishtowel, pretending she was arranging her dish towels when they entered the room.

She used to tell me all kinds of fairy tales before she got sick. I loved to go to her room and listen for hours. Now, when I looked in on her, she had her eyes closed. Pain was written on her face. I could tell she had a lot of pain. It even hurt her when I tried to touch her. I felt sad that she did not smile anymore. The pain came on more frequently and more severe; and one day in February, 1944 she died. It was a very sad day for me because I used to spend a lot of time sitting next to her bed talking to her; and now she was gone. I sobbed, "Oma... Oma... Oma. I'm going to miss you!"

She was laid out in the front room of the house in a wooden casket with sprigs of rosemary circling all around the body. It was the custom in our town to make use of the front room for funerals because it was the nicest furnished room of the house.

That night, a lot of friends and neighbors came to pray all night long until morning. The room was filled, elbow to elbow with people and even spilling out of the room into our yard down the length of our stone corridor. They were praying all night long. Next morning, the funeral procession led to the cemetery accompanied by the lonely toll of the church bell heard in the distance – ding...ding...ding.

At the grave sight the casket was lowered and, one by one, loved ones slowly passed by, throwing dirt onto the casket. As I picked up a handful of dirt to throw onto the lowered casket to say my last farewell, I felt a heavy pressure in my chest. I was overcome with sadness. Mine eyes welled with tears. It seemed my heart was tearing in pieces. Oma will not be here to tell me anymore stories. I sobbed as we started to leave.

I knew the pain of loosing a loved one; because Knoebl Opa had died suddenly of an aneurysm just a year ago, also in February. I was there when it happened and it was very frightening. Opa had been given bed rest on doctor's orders because his artery was already squeezing his voice box so that he was unable to talk. He could only whisper.

Mami periodically checked in on him to see if he had any requests because Oma already had cancer and could not take care of him. He was not even allowed to hold a glass of water.

While she was talking to him, he had a sudden urge to cough. All of a sudden, a stream of blood gushed from his mouth. Mami darted for the enameled bowl standing on the dresser next to his bed and held it under his mouth as the blood continued to pour out.

I was frozen to my spot. I could not move. Then the bleeding stopped. Opa took a handkerchief lying next to his three huge pillows that supported his back, wiped his mouth, folded the handkerchief neatly, laid it down, and then stretched out so hard with his arms and legs that the whole bed creaked. He closed his eyes and breathed no more.

I was five years old. I could not fathom what just had happened. It all happened so fast. I stood in shock; I don't remember what happened next. All I could see before me was a big lavour (enameled wash bowl) full of blood and blood all over. I can't remember anything else that happened.

The summer of 1944 was still a happy summer playing with Lisi and Franzi and my girl friends across the street. Then little by little I saw people from our town leaving on a wagon with a lot of their belongings piled on top and waving us good bye. I could not understand why they wanted to move away. I found out later that the soldiers of the retreating German Army had admonished ethnic German people to leave town because of the threat of the approaching Red Army.

Then in August, all of a sudden Dati had disappeared. Mami told us she did not know where he was. We prayed for him wherever he was and hoped he was alive. I missed Dati very much. I missed snuggling up to Dati and Mami in the evenings listening to Marlene Dietrich singing on the Radio. The house seemed so empty with Dati gone. Tettman Stefan-Vetter, Dati's business partner, also was gone. Dati's workshop was silent.

The only people now occupying our house were Urendl (great-grandma Knoebl), Mami, my eleven year old brother, Joschi and I. Plus we had two horses, a cow, our black mischievous sheep, some pigs and chickens.

Mami had a lot of responsibility on her shoulders, plus all the work of the vineyard, to take care of. Most men from our town had left to go to war. September was the deadline when all men of the town were compelled to go to war. September, 1944 arrived. Now, all schools were closed. The hustle and bustle of a happy town was gone. The town seemed empty. Grandpas and grandmas and mothers with children were the only ones left in our town of seven thousand original inhabitants.

More and more bombers were flying overhead, more frequent dashing into cellars. We children played as usual, still carefree, not having as yet felt the taste of war. But the happy time of childhood that each of us enjoyed living in peace with our neighboring towns all around us for almost 200 years soon vanished forever, never to be reclaimed again.

I was looking forward to harvesting our grapes. I loved eating grapes. A few weeks went by. The grapes were ripening. October was approaching. It started to rain. It rained real hard for three weeks continuously. The streets were a muddy mess. It was difficult to harvest the grapes. Mami abandoned the grape harvest.

Since it was now October, all the women of the town concentrated on going to the nightly prayer meetings held annually in the month of October since the founding of Sentiwan in 1763. October was dedicated as the month of Thanksgiving and prayers for God's blessings in the year ahead.

In the past during the peaceful time, Dati and Mami had volunteered to be church bell ringers in Sentiwan. That meant that whenever a fire broke out or a threatening storm was approaching, they would climb up the church steeple and pull on the ropes of the bells and pull with all their might to make the bells ring alarmingly loud. The ringing of the bells plus the blowing of the trumpet signaled a fire. Volunteer fire fighters rushed to the burning scene with their wagons equipped with barrels of water and buckets. They formed a line of people passing the filled water buckets to the fire to be extinguished. When a severe storm was threatening, the bells warned people to take cover.

Sentiwan used to be a beautiful and peaceful town to grow up in. War never touched the town, even when there was war all around, until the end of October 1944, when the Russians came through on their way to the front near Apatin. That was the beginning of the end of the ethnic German Danube Swabians, as we were called, whose ancestors had immigrated into Hungary in1763, at the request of Empress Maria Theresa to make the land productive after it had been left as wasteland by the Turks.

Part 1
Lisl's Story

My name is Elizabeth Stefan Spaltensperger, better known as Betty. I was born on Kirchweih Sunday, June 26, 1938 in Prigrevica Sveti Ivan, Yugoslavia, Province Batschka (Backa). My parents Heinrich and Elisabeth Stefan named me Elisabeth – Lisl for short. I have a brother six years older than I named Josef and called Joschi (Yoe'-shee). The provinces surrounding Batschka are: Baranja, Banat, Syrmia (Srem), and Slavonia, now known as the Voivodina, the most fertile land in Yugoslavia, located between the Danube (Donau) and Tisza (Theiss) Rivers.

There was continual rivalry between Hungary and Yugoslavia - each country trying to claim those provinces. The rivalry began in 1918 when the terms of the Treaty of Trionon awarded those Provinces to the newly formed country of Yugoslavia. Those Provinces formerly belonged to the Austria-Hungary Empire. As a result, those Provinces bounced back and forth between Hungary and Yugoslavia. The inhabitants of the towns did not take up arms and fight one another. Daily life went on as usual. The only change occurred with the officials in the town hall and some instruction in school.

All people born in these provinces before 1918 were considered Hungarian. Therefore, my parents were born in

Hungary, while I, born in the same town after 1918 was considered born in Yugoslavia.

During the Hungarian rule, both the German and Hungarian languages were taught at our schools; the German because that was the town's ethnicity, and of course Hungarian, because of the political situation. Under Hungarian rule, my town was called Bacs-Szentivan (Botch-SENteevon) in honor of John the Baptist. The meaning of the name of Bacs-Szentivan is like saying the town of St. John in the Province of Batschka. "Szent" translated saint and "ivan" translated John. The inhabitants of the town called it Sentiwan (St. John) for short.

After 1918, the town became part of Yugoslavia and was given the Serbian name, Prigrevica Sveti Ivan (PreegreVEEza SVEHTtee-eevon). "Pri"means before and "grevica"means grevice (a Roman fortification). The Serbian name explains it as the town of St. John located in front of the Roman fortification (a huge foxhole with a mountain of earth behind it. We called it Roemerschantz.) In Roman times, after a battle, all the dead- soldiers and horses- were placed into the pit and covered up with dirt for a quick burial. Many valuable items and old coins as well as skulls were dug up by children from our town who were playing in the area and found these items by accident.

Under Serbian government, the languages taught in school were German and Serbo-Croation; and the Serb Officials took over the affairs of the town hall.

The language of instruction in school was German for some 180 years. No matter what country one belonged to, either Hungary or Yugoslavia, ethnic German was spoken as the ruling language in every house.

At the time of my birth, Sentiwan was a colony of 7000 inhabitants, of pure German ethnicity that had settled there beginning in 1763. This region was colonized in response to a plea from Empress Maria Theresa of Austria who reigned as the queen of Hungary at the same time. Maria Theresa inherited the land after the death of her father, Charles VI, who was Emperor of Austria. He was the last male descendent of the Habsburg line of emperors and had been involved in a long war by the Turks over whom he was victorious.

Following the war by the Turks, the land was decimated and left as wasteland. Therefore, the Empress was anxious to re-populate the newly inherited territory to her Austria-Hungary Empire as quickly as possible.

She offered Germans a ten-year, tax-free homestead and land contracts if they would move to Hungary and build up the land and make it productive. Every family received all the farm equipment, the wagons, the horses, the cows, and all the seeds they needed for free. Many Germans in the Southeastern part of the country, who were paying high taxes considered this a great opportunity and incentive and took up the offer.

As the reigning Queen of Hungary, *Maria Theresa was seeking farmers skilled in unique farming techniques – introducing the steel plow and crop rotation to this virgin soil. She wanted various skilled tradesmen in every colony so that each colony was self-supporting and productive. Each newly married couple also received a spinning wheel when they arrived at their destination.

Since the area was low land, trenches had to be dug to drain the land in order to make their farms productive.

They dug big canals on the borderline between countries to mark the border. This process also drained the land at the same time. Many died from swamp fever the first year.

Because the land was void of trees, they built their houses from mud. Each house had a foundation of stamped mud which was sun-dried before the walls were added. They disassembled the flat-bottomed boat, used to travel down the Danube River, in order to make molds.

Next, the walls were constructed by filling big wooden molds with mud, stamping it solid, and sun-drying it before removing the boards. Then, trusses were erected and the roof covered with thick bundles of reeds, abundant in the area. The reeds made it leak proof. The walls of the mud houses were two feet thick and eight feet high with window ledges on the inside about two feet deep so that one could sit on the window ledge and look out the window. Because the walls were so thick, it did not take much wood to heat the house in the winter.

When the mud house was finished, it was white washed inside and out. Some folks tinted their inside walls either a pale green or a pale yellow. The walls on the inside were just as smooth as our modern day drywall. Some walls even had floral stenciling that looked like floral wall paper. My maternal grandparents, the Knoebls, owned an original mud-stamped house but replaced the reed-covered roof with a tile roof. The front room of the house had beautiful stencil floral patterns on the walls. I know this to be true, because I lived in my Knoebl grandparents' house for five years until we were expelled from their house by Tito's Partisaner. A lot of the houses that were built in 1763 were still in good condition in 1945 when we were evacuated.

As time went by and the town began to grow, two brick yards were built in Sentiwan and then people began building their houses with brick and replaced the reed covered roofs with tile.

The deep holes created all over the town when building the mud houses, drained the farm lands; and in time turned those excavations into ponds – for swimming in summer and ice skating in winter. It took two more years of hard work before the land showed productivity.

Everyone worked hard to make a good future for their families; because they were not burdened by taxes. Only when the family was well established, taxes were collected. The settlers began to prosper after three years of sweat and hard work. They took pride in what they had accomplished. People were content and happy, thanking God for giving them the opportunity for a brand new start in life.

They kept their German code of dress and clung to the customs of their homeland. However, in time, they developed a unique, new language, using various words from the Hungarian language as well as the Serbo-Croation, and incorporated those words with the German language. As a result, the Danube Swabian dialect was born. This language is unique because people coming directly from Germany would not be able to understand what was spoken. For instance: "Good morning" in proper German is "Guten Morgen" but "Gudi Mar-ya" in the new dialect. The word "hinauf" (to go up) is shortened to "nuf." Every German word is shortened quite a bit – with a few Hungarian and Serbo-Croation words peppered in – here and there. When people introduced themselves, the family name was always said first followed by the given name. For instance:

My name is Spaltensperger, Betty. What is yours?

My father's ancestors came from Alsace-Lorraine - it was on the French border in Germany. Family name "Stefan," Johann a barrel maker, immigrated to Batschsentiwan in May, 1764.

My mother's ancestors, "Knoebl" Johann, a shoemaker, came from the Black Forest (Schwarzwald); and they also settled in Batschsentiwan.

In 1767, the town already had 235 houses.

The farmers turned this barren land into very fertile farm land and it became known as the "Bread Basket" of Yugoslavia. The people that had settled in the Voivodina region became known as the "Danube Swabians."

*Marie Antoinette was the daughter of Empress Maria Theresa of Austria.

Chapter 1
What's a Russ Doing Here?

October in Sentiwan, from the time the first German ancestors arrived in 1763, has always been a month dedicated to observing of nightly prayer meetings the entire month. This was such a night that left a permanent piece of history in my mind at the age of six. It was one night in October, 1944 that my mother – I called her Mami – was getting ready to go to prayer. Prayers of Thanksgiving for the past bountiful harvest were uttered as well as prayers for good health, for peace among neighbors and for all of God's blessings.

Mami stood in front of the mirror combing her hair when I entered the bedroom. I walked across the room and sat at the edge of our bed and watched her as she pulled the comb over and through her pretty black hair. I thought Mami was beautiful. Then she stopped and put the comb down. Taking a second glance at her reflection in the mirror, turned around and said, "Lisl, behave while I'm gone. Don't give Urendl (great-grandma, Knoebl) any trouble." I promised Mami.

We both stepped out the door. Then I leaned against the door post and watched her walk cheerfully down the corridor and out the front gate. I was still standing there wondering what to do next when the front gate flew open and Mami darted back into the yard with a very frightened expression on her face. She slammed the wooden gate shut, locked it, and braced her back against the gate. She took a deep breath and words just blurted from her lips, "A Russ! Uf dr Gass is a Russ."

In the meantime, Urendl came slowly walking down the long corridor yelling, "Du bischt noch do?" "You're still here? I thought you were already gone. Aren't you going to be late?" When she came closer and saw the frightened expression on Mami's face she asked, "Was is los?" "What's the matter? You look like you've just seen a ghost."

Mami replied, "Uf dr Gass is a Russ, mit om'e G'wer. Was dut dan a Russ do?" Translated: "A Russian officer is walking down the street with a gun over his shoulder. What's a Russian officer doing in Sentiwan?" They both looked puzzled.

Mami was still leaning with her back to the gate, as if to re-enforce it so no one could enter, waiting. She wasn't quite sure what to do. She tried to muster up enough courage to open the gate and peek out. She turned around and, oh so carefully, lifted the latch and peeked out. The Russian officer was nowhere in sight; and everything seemed normal. Therefore, she decided to go and waved us good bye.

Urendl and I strode slowly down the long brick walkway to her room. The roof of the house extended over the long corridor from front to back so that one could walk from room to room without getting wet. Urendl's room was the fourth door down the corridor. One could enter each family's room only from the outside (like a motel).

Urendl was already 80 years old and walked quite slowly. We barely made it to her door when we heard the sound of thunder in the distance.

"Aw," Urendl said in disgust, "not more rain. For three weeks it has rained and the streets are already a muddy mess." But the thundering sound went on and on. There was no lightening and no rain, but the heavy rumble continued and we felt the earth trembling under our feet. Urendl thought it was strange.

When Mami came back from prayer, she said the sound we heard was the sound of Stalin's Orgel, Russia's powerful multi-barrel cannon and the war was coming closer.

"The stained glass windows rattled and the earth beneath our feet trembled so much during prayer that all the women were terribly frightened," said Mami. "In fact, the priest went up into the pulpit to try to calm us down." He said, "Don't be afraid. The cannon is far away and it will not touch us. There was war before; and it did not touch us. Don't be afraid."

What Mami told us eased our minds.

Soon thereafter we went to bed. I did not like to hear that "thunder" sound. It did not seem to bother my twelve year old brother, Joschi, too much. Boys are much tougher than girls. I did not like loud noises; and therefore, I had a hard time falling asleep.

In the morning I was awakened by loud yelling and cursing in Russian. I heard the sound of whips and horses whimpering and snorting. It sounded like someone was beating a horse. I was about to jump out of bed to get dressed and go outside to see what was going on. Just then Mami came into the room with a very frightened look on her face and told Joschi and me to get dressed but stay inside. After I put on my dress, Mami attempted to braid my hair when a loud knock came on our front gate and a Russian voice demanded, "Open up!"

Mami gave me and Joschi a "stay put" sign and went quickly to unlock the gate. Several Russian soldiers came storming into our house and nearly knocked her down. To our surprise, some of the Russian soldiers were women! The soldiers went from room to room throughout the whole house, looking at everything and taking whatever they wanted. They acted like they owned the place.

When they saw our beds with the down comforters on top, they lay down on the white comforters with their muddy boots. I saw Mami's face cringe. She was frozen to the spot in fear. Joschi and I stood mute, afraid to move.

The women soldiers went into our front room and snooped through our armoire and helped themselves to Mami's beautiful dress-up clothes. Whatever they liked, they took. All three of us stood there frightened and helpless. They left the yard with their arms full of Mami's favorite things. The room was in disarray with clothes thrown all over the floor. Mami always had the house neat and clean; but when they left the house, every room was a muddy mess. Their actions scared the wits out of me.

After they left our yard, I heard a lot of commotion on the street. Out of curiosity, I wanted to see what was happening; but I was too frightened to go outside after what I had just witnessed in our house. I went into our front room which had a window view to the street. I stood behind the lace curtains and peeked out.

There were a lot of wagons on our street, one behind the other, as far as I could see. The wheels of the wagons were mired hub-deep in the muddy road and the uniformed men cracked their whips against the flanks of the horses again and again trying to make them pull the wagons out. But nothing budged. The horses just could not pull the wagons out of the mud with all that ammunition piled on top of the wagons. The Russian soldiers pilfered in every house and terrorized the citizens of the whole town.

Last week Mami had heard a rumor from some women at the prayer meetings that the Russians came through the Province of Banat on their way to the front, looted the whole town and carried away a lot of their belongings. This rumor caused Mami to gather a lot of our best things and hide them up in the attic of our summer kitchen as soon as she heard about it in case the Red Army would pass through our town, also.

The attic above our summer kitchen had an entry that was so concealed that no one could tell that there was a door. I'm glad she thought of doing that otherwise our linens and towels and other nice things would have been taken.

The inhabitants of the whole town were relieved when the mud dried in the street and the Red Army moved on and things were back to normal.

Chapter 2
Russians Invade Sentiwan

On November 1, 1944, Russian soldiers along with Tito's Partisans came marching into our town and occupied it. They celebrated their victory by drinking whatever they could find to drink. They liberated Yugoslavia from occupation by Hungary that had occurred at Easter, 1941 when Hitler bombed Belgrade. Tito of Yugoslavia and Stalin of Russia had made an agreement. If Russia helped Tito and his Partisans regain the land that Hungary occupied in 1941, then Tito, in exchange, would give Russia slave laborers for the rebuilding of Russia's war damaged country.

The Russians ransacked our homes, took anything they wanted and brutalized the inhabitants. Upon their arrival, the inhabitants of the town were compelled to share their house with the soldiers and give them food and lodging after they returned from their mission of daily bombings.

Usually evenings in our town were quiet until 11:00 p.m., the time when the Russians returned from the airport after landing their bombers. There was a three kilometer walk from the airstrip to Sentiwan. Because the soldiers were already intoxicated before they arrived, havoc began as soon as they set foot in town.

They broke into the houses looking for fun and violated the women. In their drunken state anything in their mind was licit. They used to steal chickens and roosters on their way back from the airport and brought them to one's house and demanded the woman of that house cook the chickens for supper.

Because the women first had to kill and pluck the chickens, it was a long process before they could eat. This gave them plenty of opportunity for searching and plundering one's home, and looking for things the owner might have hidden. When a hiding place was found, then the owner was brutally beaten for hiding things from them.

To provide food for the winter, almost every household in Sentiwan killed a pig. This day was called Schlachtfest. Slaughtering a pig was usually done in the middle of November and again around New Years. In our household, the day of the Schlachtfest was November 19, the "names day" for "Elisabeth," because Mami and I and my cousin Schneider Lisi were all named Elisabeth. Therefore, we had a big family celebration. It was customary in our Province of Batschka to celebrate the "names day" of a person not one's birthday.

Relatives and friends were invited and all helped with processing the pig. The pig's bladder was cleaned and filled up with water like a water balloon for children to play with. Children had lots of fun tossing it around from one to another like tossing water balloons.

Hams and bacon and Bratwurst were prepared and smoked to keep them from spoiling. I especially liked the cracklings (Grammeln). They were one inch cubed chunks of back fat that were deep fried to a golden brown and eaten like French fries with salt sprinkled over them. They were crispy and crunchy – yummmmm.

The evening meal for all guests included "Wurst Soup" and roasted Bratwurst, pork roast, and fresh baked bread. Then the evening came to a finale with everyone sitting in a circle singing our favorite songs.

However, there was no Schlachtfest celebration in November, 1944, when the Russians came and occupied our town. In fact there were no more celebrations of any kind from then on.

The Russian soldiers broke into the houses to look for good things to eat. They took whatever they wanted and often left the owners almost without anything - all that hard work and now nothing to show for it - gone in an instant. Wheat, potatoes, cattle corn, and winter squash were the only staples left to carry us through winter.

When the townsfolk saw how the Russians broke into the houses and kept taking the hams, bacon, and Bratwurst without hesitation, almost everyone started to hide their goods.

Urendl made a comment one day and praised Mami for having the foresight to hide all her favorite things way back in October when she had heard the rumor of soldiers looting in the Province of Banat. Urendl said, "They will never find the secret hiding place in the attic above our summer kitchen. Your husband did a good job with his woodworking skill. There's no door to be seen." Mami agreed.

Ever since the Russians occupied our town, it was a time of hiding. Night time was dreaded. The troops violated women in their seventies as well as little girls. In the evenings no lights were lit in our house because Mami wanted to make it look like no one lived here.

Often we slept at our neighbor's house. Although Burghardt Leopold Vetter was an old man, Mami felt safer by us staying with him and his wife as opposed to the three of us alone in our house. We slept in different places on different nights.

We were afraid to sleep in our bedroom so Mami, Joschi and I, all three of us, slept in one bed in our summer kitchen that was located next to Dati's work shop. That way, if they broke into our bedroom at night, they would find it empty and believe no one was home. The bedrooms and regular kitchen were located on the opposite side of the yard.

I remember one particular night, a night that I will never forget. Mami, Joschi and I had all gone to bed in our summer kitchen when suddenly we were startled by sounds coming from the front of the house, sounds of drunken men hollering and singing. There was no time to hide. Before we knew what was what, twenty soldiers came stumbling into our kitchen as though they had just materialized from thin air. They were drunk and demanded that my mother serve them supper while they attempted to seat themselves around the kitchen table, staggering and tripping over their own feet. During the commotion, Mami told Joschi, "Run, go to Milan, for help!" Unnoticed, Joschi ran out the door and on to the police station. Milan, the Chief of Police, was a Serb who had been a good friend of ours for many years.

There were so many of them. I was terrified. Mami hurried to the cellar, taking me with her, to fetch smoked Bratfwurst and several loaves of bread. Bratwurst was something that did not take long to cook. She put them in a big pot and placed it on the cooking plate of our big, brown ceramic cooking hearth. Then she proceeded to slice up several loaves of freshly baked bread and piled it on a plate. As she hustled to put food on the table, one of the senior men, or at least one who seemed to carry some authority with the rest, scooped me up and sat me on his lap. Suddenly as if on cue, they all drew their pistols and began to shoot into the ceiling, laughing. I was terribly frightened. I covered my ears and started to scream. The more I screamed, the louder they laughed. This was my first exposure to gunfire and the noise was unbearable. I was frightened beyond reason. The two young soldiers sitting across the table laughing uproariously as the slightly older commandant, on whose lap I had been forced to sit, drunkenly emptied his pistol into the ceiling.

Mami was frozen to her spot at the stove. She knew any reaction on her part would be just an excuse for the pistol's barrel to be lowered. If she could stay calm and pretend it was just another evening supper being served by a gracious hostess to invited guests, the soldiers would go away after their appetite was served. Mami piled the Bratwurst on a platter and placed it on the table. The officer eventually tired of me and let me go to reach for food. Then they all started eating.

As soon as he let me go, I slid off his lap, ran out the kitchen, and darted across the yard heading straight to our bedroom. I jumped into our bed and pulled the down comforter, over my head. My fright and trembling kept me from falling asleep. The shooting and revelry seemed never ending.

Suddenly I heard shooting in the yard. I heard the sound of bullets hitting various places of the house. I lay in bed terrified. Then little by little the laughing, hollering and shooting faded into the distance.

When Joschi finally arrived with Milan, the soldiers were already gone and everything was quiet.

The next morning, we found bullet holes all over our house and even in the wall of our neighbor, Horn Kathi-Bas' house. Then we headed across the yard and stepped into our summer kitchen. "What a sight!" When I looked at Mami, I could tell she was heart broken. There was debris all over the floor and table from the ruined ceiling. What a mess! Mami checked her special things, she had stored in the attic overhead, to keep them from getting looted. Everything was full of holes, nothing salvageable. It was a sad day for Mami because all our nice things were destroyed with bullet holes; but it was also a good day – we were all alive and unharmed. "Gott sei Dank!" (God be thanked!)

Toward the end of November 1944, we heard a familiar sound, "Ra-ta-ta-ta-ta-da- ratatata-ta-ta-da." The drummer, the town crier, marched through Sentiwan announcing that he had a message from the government. Everyone needed to come and hear the new law that went into effect November 21, 1944, at Jajce, Bosnia.

Announcements by the drummer were almost a daily occurrence now. When the Russians occupied our town, everyone who owned a radio had to give it up and bring it to the town square for the use of the Russian army. But now, to hear the news of the day, everyone strictly had to rely on the message from the town crier.

The announcement declared that all ethnic Germans born in Yugoslavia were stripped of their citizenship and all homes, farms, vineyards, cattle, and any other good would be confiscated and given to the Serbs. The inhabitants of Sentiwan were upset and worried about what was announced; but the women had no one they could talk to – their men were all gone to war. No one knew what that message all entailed.

From then on, little by little families of Serbs moved into different houses in town; and the inhabitants had to share their house with them and even had to cook for them.

In one house, a family of Serbs with many young children moved in and made the previous owner of the house cook a kettle full of food for them. When it was cooked, they placed the kettle on the floor with the entire family circled around the kettle, sitting on the floor with legs crisscrossed. Then they reached in with their hands and ate without using plates or silverware.

In another house, a family moved in and built a fire in the middle of the bedroom that had no chimney; and the walls of that room were black with soot, in no time. We knew they were not used to living in houses.

When Christmas season came, we did not bake any cookies like we used to before the Russians came. They robbed us of all the necessary items needed. Besides, most stores were closed or running out of goods. One had to get by with what one had in the larder. We dared not do anything. We constantly had to be on guard, and be prepared to hide. I was disappointed that we could not celebrate Christmas. I missed Dati. I wondered where he was and hoped he was safe. Our whole family used to sit around the Christmas tree singing our favorite carols. We all loved to sing. Not just at Christmas time, but also at corn shucking time and at "knitting and spinning-wool parties." I wished with all my heart that life was back to normal. But things went from bad to worse.

Chapter 3
Robota!

Two days after Christmas, again the drummer marched throughout town, summoning young men age seventeen to forty-five and women age seventeen to thirty to appear at the Sportsplatz (soccer field) by noon for "Robota" (work). Mami went to see what was happening. I was told to stay with Urendl till she came back. When Mami came back, she told Urendl, "The Russians selected 200 young men and women for work duty. They will be sent far away, by train. They were not told where they were sending them, but probably for one month."

Urendl replied, "One month is a long time to be sent away to work, especially in the winter. I wonder what kind of work that will be and what kind of clothes they will need to take?"

Mami went on, "They selected women eighteen years old on up to thirty. I'm lucky. I'm thirty- two, so I don't have to go. Even my niece, Brettraeger Nandl, and her husband, were among them that were on the list."

Mami was silent for a moment and then she continued, "You know what bothers me the most? They selected mothers who had small children with them because they had no grandparents to care for them. Those children were given to strangers to care for them until they returned."

Urendl replied, "That is awful!" "That goes to show you, in war, anything goes."

When I heard their conversation, I was sure glad that they didn't take Mami. I felt real sorry for those little ones who were given to strangers. I thought to myself, "I don't think that I could bear it if I would have been given to strangers to live with. I'm so shy that I blush when a stranger even just looks at me. I'm sooo glad Mami is thirty-two years old.

The next few days were sad days in our town, because the two hundred young folks were taken away by Russian soldiers. They marched them out of town, at gun point, to the district railroad station in the town of Apatin. The parents of those young folk, being sent away, and the little children left behind with strangers were not even allowed to hug or kiss them when they left. Everyone was in tears as they watched them fade into the distance.

There were still some young folk locked up in the Jugendheim building after the group was marched away because the Russian officers were undecided, whether or not to take those seventeen year olds to Russia for hard labor.

The following is an account of what happened to seventeen year old young men and seventeen year old young women from Sentiwan who were rounded up at the Sportsplatz for work duties on the day the group of two hundred were chosen for ROBOTA.

The Russians decided the last minute **not** to take those seventeen years old. One had to appear at the Sportsplatz if one's birthday was close to eighteen. During the commotion of that day, some seventeen year olds were locked up by mistake.

I have a friend named Barbara Mueller Ottenthal who was rounded up with the young folk on December 27 and locked up in the Jugendheim building. (a building for youth activities like YMCA). She was seventeen years old at that time and she told me what happened to the ones they took by mistake.

Barbara told me, "We were locked up overnight in the Jugendheim building, heavily guarded. We were waiting to be bussed to the railroad station in Apatin the following morning.

As one entered the building, there was a ten foot square vestibule. French doors divided the vestibule from the main hall. To the right side of the vestibule was a room which the Russian officers used as their office.

I could speak the Serbo-Croation language very well; and I overheard the Russian officers saying that they were not taking anyone born in 1927; therefore excluding those who were seventeen years old."

Barbara continued, "I had a few friends with me, also only seventeen years old; but they could not speak the Serbian language. When I mentioned to them what I overheard, they persuaded me to go to the Russian officers and ask to be released.

I attempted to do that. However, Tito's Partisans, who were in charge of guarding the group, went after me pulled me back and would not let me see the Russian Officer.

All night long I tried to think of a way I could let the Russian Officer know that a few were only 17 years old; but I did not have the opportunity.

In the morning, we were lined up to be ushered onto the bus. My father was already seated on the bus because he was among the ones chosen for the work detail. I was not permitted to speak to him because women were separated from the men. One of my girl friends, Paitz Wabschl (Barbara), had already been seated on the bus.

As the line crept up and I reached the French doors, I suddenly dropped my backpack and quickly threw myself into the office, where the Russian officers were seated. I lost my balance and ran into the officer's desk so hard that I broke my aluminum "Herrgott's ring." I managed to get their attention though; and, as a result two were freed, beside myself, and were allowed to go home. However, I could not persuade them to release my friend Wabschl already seated on the bus."

Barbara continued, "From then on all the young folk from our town between twelve years old and seventeen had to go daily to the airport, three kilometers from Sentiwan, to load bombs onto Russian planes.

Since it was winter and I did not have any boots, I wore "klumpa" (wooden shoes) filled with straw to keep my feet from freezing. The Russians were kind to us girls and gave us a hand when they noticed us struggling with the weight of the bombs. They did not help the young men though. This routine went on for one month until the end of January, 1945.

When the work of loading the bombs was finished, we were sent to Apatin to the shores of the Danube to dig trenches for the protection of the Russian soldiers who were fighting the German army who had a stronghold across the Danube River. While we were digging, Russian and German bombers flew overhead; but we were never in any danger.

We worked from 5:00 a.m. daily until 11:00 p.m. and received only one bowl of soup per day with just a little something in it. That was all we received – nothing else. They did not give us any water to drink while we were digging. We were desperate for a drink of water. So desperate that we scooped up the water that had collected in the horses' hoof prints and drank it.

We slept in a huge building somewhere along the shores of the Danube River with straw on the floor. The building had no windows or doors; and therefore it was very cold and drafty. I became ill with diphtheria. I had very swollen tonsils and developed a very high fever. I couldn't walk because I was too weak to walk.

Because I could no longer work, they sent me to the death camp Gakowa. I was placed in a room with 25 other sick people. Every morning, two or three in our room were found dead. Because I could hardly breathe with my badly swollen tonsils, they put me into a barn with the dead that had died during the night.

The Partisans used to come into the barn to check the dead; and poked me with their bayoneted rifle to check if I was alive or not. I did not want to look at them so I closed my eyes when they entered; but I could hear every word they were saying. I heard them say, "She is not dead yet."

When they left, two little old ethnic German ladies, also internees in Gakowa's Death Camp came with chicory tea and forced me to drink it, trying to help me get better. It was very, very bitter. They put the rest of the steamed herb on a rag and laid it on my stomach and chest.

I also had a big boil in the hollow of my left elbow. The boil had a tiny hole. When I pressed on it, puss squirted out. I had another boil on my left hand between the little finger and the ring finger. It was so badly infected that one could see raw flesh.

One of the little old ladies caught a frog, cut it in half and put the inner parts of the frog on each boil and wrapped it up. I was too sick to object to their treatment. The inner parts of the frog pulled out all the infection in both boils and each one healed. I could not believe it; but it worked. I had not heard anything like that done on a boil before.

When I got better, the two little old ladies helped me back into the room I previously occupied. They continued giving me that bitter chicory tea and brought me my daily ration of soup and cared for me.

I recovered nicely; and when I was well, I was taken to the town of Siwatz nearby to work on a farm. One day, all of us workers on the farm were sitting on the ground eating our lunch. The women were sitting together in a long row; and across from us women, the men were also sitting in along row, eating their lunch.

One of the men sitting across from me wore over- the-knee, wide-legged white pants made from hemp. Those were customary garb worn by farmers in the summer who worked in the hot sun all day because the material was strong and cool. They looked like baggy shorts but over the knee length.

We were eating and talking. I stopped talking for a moment to take a bite of my lunch. As I raised my head and looked across, I noticed a mouse running up one pant leg and coming out the other one from the man sitting across from me. I was shocked and held my breath seeing the mouse run in and out, waiting for his reaction.

Suddenly, startled, he jumped to his feet. "What the.........!" he yelled. It happened so fast, he had no idea what had gotten into his pants. I yelled, "A mouse! A mouse!" When all saw the mouse run, we had a good laugh, till our belly hurt. Amongst all the misery we endured, sometimes there was an occasional moment of humor.

While spending ten months as a slave laborer in Russia, my father became ill. He was one of the two hundred who was sent there for the rebuilding of war damaged Russia.

Russia released one transport of sick workers and sent them to a farm. It was a one time only transport of the sick back to their homeland. I don't know where he was sent after he was released, but he recovered there.

After he got better, he tried to find my mom and me because he had heard what Tito and his Partisaner did to the ethnic Germans. He sneaked in and out of several death camps in Yugoslavia trying to find us. He had no idea of our whereabouts. It was very risky for him to do that.

Finally he sneaked into the Death Camp Gakowa where my mother and I were. By asking questions of people if they knew anyone from the town of Sentiwan, he eventually found us both and then planned for a way to escape.

My father, Mueller Hans, was a courageous man and planned a successful escape for his family from the Death Camp Gakowa."

The above story gives us a tiny glimpse of the life experiences of the youth twelve years old on up to seventeen, from our beloved town of Sentiwan, who were used for slave labor by Tito's Partisan soldiers in Yugoslavia 1944-1947.

Chapter 4
Tito's Partisaner Take Over

After the Russian soldiers left Sentiwan with the group of two hundred young men and women, they marched them to Apatin and loaded them onto cattle wagons and hauled them away. Word came January 2, 1945, that they were sent to Russia.

When the Russians were gone, Tito's "Partisans" moved in. They were the ones now in charge.

They came with big sacks and also went throughout our houses and plundered our closets and took the beautiful satin and velvet jackets, the garb worn by the women of our town. What the Russian women soldiers left behind after plundering, Tito's Partisan soldiers now took. If they happened to like a pair of boots or any other item of clothing one wore, one had to give it up at once. One could not refuse them.

My father had given my brother a real nice fur cap for the oncoming winter when Dati was still at home. When the Partisans took over, one came along and simply took my brother's fur cap right off his head and left him without one. That was a sad moment for my brother. They were very brutal. One had to carry out their wishes at an instant or be brutally beaten. Many old men were knocked down and kicked with their hobnail boots. They had no respect for the elderly. They loved to see blood flow.

Our carefree childhood days of playing with our friends were over. The arrival of Tito's Partisans signaled a frightening time for women and girls. Mothers instructed their daughters to stay out of sight of any of the "Partisaner" as Mami called them. "If you see a Partisaner, run and hide. Whatever you do, don't get caught! They will do monstrous things to you."

Doors were always kept locked and no one dared venture into the street alone. When children wanted to go play with their friends, they'd go out the back way through the garden, first looking to make sure no soldiers were in sight, then dash out and run for cover, repeating this behavior several times until they reached the safety of their friends' homes.

I had a girlfriend named Frank Rosi who was a little older and taller than I was. When Rosi and I were playing and heard the Partisans knocking at the front gate of the house, we would run and jump out the window and dash into the garden and hide in the bushes. She would jump first and then catch me because I was too scared to jump that far down by myself.

We knew instinctively that our young age was no protection. There was no age limit to the Partisans' lusty, roving eyes. They violated five year old little girls and women in their 70's. It gave them pleasure to see horror on our faces. It was hard to believe that only a few months before we had been playing our childhood games without a care in our young lives. Oh how we longed for those days again. Many of my friends died in the concentration camp.

It was midnight on March 11, 1945, when the sound of the drum again was heard as the drummer marched throughout the streets. We had already been sleeping and were awakened by the beat of the drum. Everyone rushed out of their house running down the street to the corner, the spot where the drummer called out his message,

"Everyone pack food for six days for each person and bring it with you and assemble in the town square within two hours. Every single person in town must be assembled. Old, young, sick, well. No exceptions! Anyone refusing to come will be shot on the spot! Those fit for work also bring a shovel or a rake."

That was a tall order for such short notice, since we were just awakened from sleep. There was a lot of hustle and bustle in each household. Getting dressed as quickly as possible was number one. What to bring in the way of food that would last for six days without spoiling was a major concern. Mothers rushed around gathering food items and checking what was left in the larder to make sure there was enough for the children's bundles. There was no time to prepare anything. Whatever bread was left in the cellar had to be divided among family members.

When the Russians came and occupied our town, the marauding soldiers confiscated all the smoked hams and sausage that the towns' people had stored up for the winter. There was not much left that could be brought without cooking it first. I watched as Mami frantically tried to gather and pack enough food for Joschi and me. All she was able to gather up was smoked bacon, which she retrieved from her hiding place, and bread. It was a good thing that Mami had just baked some bread that morning. She wrapped each person's food in a clean dish towel and tied it at the four corners so it would be easy to carry. We each had our bundle of food. Mami took a Rucksack (Backpack).

When I asked, "why do we have to rush around like this in the middle of the night?" Mami's answer was, "I don't know."

Grownups had backpacks and children little bundles. Families were rushing out of their houses. Off, everyone went in family groups to the town square. The question on every one's mind, "Why at this time of night?"

There were about one hundred of Tito's armed Partisan soldiers carrying out various orders. Some were separating the people, some searching houses for people reluctant to leave. Some Partisan soldiers were leading away the men that had been imprisoned. As we arrived in the town square, the Partisans released seventy-five male prisoners with shovel in hand, lined them up, four men in a row, and marched them out of town taking the road that lead to Sombor. Dati was among them.

Those men were the men who had survived the bombings by the Russians and walked home when the Hungarian army was decimated. When they arrived in town, Tito's Partisans rounded them up and locked them in the boy's school building and held them as Tito's prisoners. Family members were not allowed to visit them. When they marched them out of Sentiwan, no one knew where they were taken.

When we were all assembled in the square, some Partisans ordered all the elderly to assemble on one side and others directed all the pregnant women and women with nursing babies to assemble on the opposite side. Women fit for hard work, carrying rakes and shovels, were put in another group. And then the melee started. No one could have foreseen the heartrending scene that was before them.

The Partisans approached the women with children and attempted to yank the children away from their mothers. The children started to scream, "Mami! Mami!" and would not let go of their grip, clinging desperately to their mother's clothes trying to hold on. The soldiers ruthless pulled them away. This action caused the children to scream even louder still reaching out and stomping with their feet continuously screaming, "Mami! Mami!" Partisans dragged them and shoved them toward the group of seniors. There were hundreds of children screaming.

My paternal grandparents, Stefan Johann and Rosalia, quickly took hold of my brother and me and both my cousins, Schneider Lisi and Franzi. The children who had no one were put with strangers.

What a sad night, children endlessly screaming wanting the comfort of their mother's arms - to no avail.

There were four hundred women fit for hard work, lined up, with their backpacks of food and their shovels or rakes. Partisans with bayonet rifles in hand surrounded them and escorted them away.

When the children saw them leaving, their screaming increased all the more, stomping their feet, and reaching desperately for their mothers. As I observed what was happening and how brutal everyone was being treated by the Partisans, I knew enough not to scream, it would have been useless.

A feeling of forsakeness came over our entire remaining family and we all sobbed as our parents were taken away. It was a heartbreaking scene. No one knew where they were going or what was to happen to them. It was 4:00 a.m. when they were marched away on the street leading to the town of Apatin.

After the women had left, the remaining people were herded into the school buildings located in the middle of town. There was a cloister school for girls and a separate school building for boys. We were locked up for three days, sitting on the floor and slept huddled together. It was so crowded we could not stretch out to sleep. We were not allowed to go outdoors the entire time.

Chapter 5
Driven From Our Homes

On March 15, 1945, we were marched out of town in a column of people numbering about three thousand five hundred, escorted by armed Partisan soldiers with bayonet rifles. We didn't know where we were going. Every now and then glancing back at the town, it did not look like our town. Looking down any street just a few days before, showed a neat, well kept town. Gates were always locked to keep dogs from roaming. But today it looked like we were walking through a ghost town - empty streets with a lot of gates left wide open as people had rushed, three days before, trying to get to the town square on time.

Seeing the gates left wide open, drew my thoughts now to my dog, "Scheckl". I was wondering what would happen to him. I'm sure Mami closed the front gate to our house because if it wasn't locked securely, he would sneak out and find Mami and me where ever we were. When we went to worship on Sundays and the gate was not locked securely, he would sneak out a few minutes later, walk into the church building and sit right down next to us where we were kneeling during worship and stay there till worship was over.

Mami's displeased facial expressions and whispered orders for him to leave and go back home were useless.

"HE STAYED!" He got his name because he was black and brown and white, with one ear black and the other one brown. He was a shorthaired mutt with a stub tail, a medium sized dog, but very smart. Who would take care of him now and who would give him fresh water? We were gone from home already three days. I did not even have a chance to pet him before we left. We had no idea things would turn out this way.

Among my family being evacuated was my Stefan Opa and Oma, my Urendl, (great grandma Knoebl Regina), my brother Joschi and I, plus both my cousins, Schneider Lisi and Franzi and their paternal grandmother, and their cousin Kuebler Anni. Lisi, Franzi, Anni, and I walked closely near our grandparents. Joschi walked with his friends nearby.

The column of people was marched out of town past the steam grain mill (where people from all over the area came to grind their wheat into flour) and onto the road leading to the town of Stapari, which was a Serbian town. We did not know where they were taking us. We just walked and walked and walked, all day long, with hardly any rest.

I remember it was a beautiful sunny March day. A day that usually would have seen us playing ball and "Fange-les" (tag), and "Higle" (hopscotch) or just basking in the sunshine after a long winter indoors. The violets were already blooming.

I was wearing my blue wool coat, a dress, long, knit stockings, and carrying my bundle of food. The sun was shining as we were walking, and the warm rays were penetrating our coats. We were getting overheated. We had no water with which to quench our thirst. I unbuttoned my coat; but as we walked on, the heat of the sun became stronger.

The Partisans were yelling at us, "Davai, Davai!" (Move it, move it). We were not walking fast enough to suit them. It was difficult for the very old people to keep up. The women that were pregnant and the young mothers that were carrying their little ones had a hard time. Their arms got tired from carrying their babies. When strangers offered to help carry their babies, the little ones screamed, wanting only their mothers to carry them.

One could not stop to rest, not even a moment. One had to keep up with the soldiers' tempo or get beaten or shot. It was a scary time for everyone. One never knew from moment to moment what the Partisans were going to do. They did not hesitate to shoot someone down in cold blood or beat someone to death. They loved to see blood flow.

The sunshine soon became burdensome, draining every bit of energy we had left. No one had any water to drink, except the Partisans who carried flasks of water attached to their belt. We had no idea that we were forced to leave our homes and made to walk as far as we did, and why?

I was so thirsty and sweated. I had a real urge to ditch my coat; but I couldn't. I couldn't say "Mami, please! Will you carry my coat?" There was no Mami. Where was she? Where did they take her? Where was Dati? Is he still alive?

I couldn't ask Oma to carry my coat. She did all she could to help little Franzi, four and a half years old, to keep on walking. He cried and cried and wanted Oma to carry him because he was too tired to walk. That was impossible; because she carried her rucksack over her shoulders and also Franzi's bundle of food. Besides, she was already over sixty two years old and tired herself. After all, we had been walking for hours. He had no alternative but to walk. Everyone was tired.

Many older folks ditched items of clothing and threw their shoes into the ditch because they developed blisters on their feet; and they were just too weary to carry things.

Oh! How much I hoped for the sight of shade from a tree; but there was none. A large crowd, all the old people and children, pregnant women, and women with nursing babies from our village of Sentiwan were walking along on a dry and dusty dirt road – the road which the farmers took when they went to their fields. We were guarded on each side and in the rear by Partisan soldiers armed with bayonet rifles, their eyes filled with scorn for this group of German people who never caused any harm and had lived in peace for 200 years with its Hungarian and Slavic neighbors. They were constantly yelling, "Davai! Davai!" (Move it, move it). They were repeatedly cussing and cursing.

There was not an inkling of hatred from our Slavish neighbors before this event; and now this utter look of disdain in their eyes toward us was hard to understand. Seeing the cruel mistreatment they used, made one try to keep up even if one could hardly take another step.

We came near the town of Stapari, a predominantly Serbian town, and we were hopeful that we finally would get some water in town. The people of Stapari used to be friendly to us in times past and had rented out their farm land to farmers in Sentiwan and shared profits. But when we entered the town, the people greeted us with cursing and threw stones at us and yelled, "Begei Svabo! Tito's plan is to get rid of you."

Ethnic Germans in Yugoslavia began to be hated because of the atrocities committed by Hitler's army during occupation in Yugoslavia. Even though this group of the elderly and children were innocent, we were found guilty simply because we were of German descent. That hostile greeting with a shower of rocks made many a person duck to avoid getting injured and dashed any hope of receiving that precious water.

We pressed on and passed the outskirt of town and resumed our walking. Soon the heat of the sun finally also reached down on our escorts; and they also began to slow down a bit. We came to a grove of trees and they decided to take a break. We finally got to sit and rest.

We opened our bundle of food and started to nibble a bit. There was not much left. We could not eat all we wanted because we did not know how many days we would be traveling. When we observed them drinking out of their flasks and their glee knowing that we did not have any water made us feel down trodden and weary. But it was so good to sit awhile and give our feet a break.

Then they ordered us to line up and resume our marching. We had to assist older people to rise. They were too exhausted to make it on their own. The rays of the sun seemed to get hotter. If only we could have just one sip of cool water. Everyone was plodding along. Looking ahead, the road seemed endless. How long till we reach a place to stay put? How long?

A huge cloud of dust from the endless shuffling and dragging of tired feet encircled and accompanied us. Drops of sweat gathered on our foreheads and soon the dust and sweat clung to every inch of our skin. We were caked in it.

In the distance we suddenly saw what appeared to be a farmer's well. Hope sprung up within us at the possibility of a long awaited drink of cool water to quench our dry, parched lips. The tempo of our walk increased and every muscle in our body was pushed to its limit. But our hope soon was crushed. When we arrived at the well, the Partisans drank cool water and filled up their canteens; but they denied us any water and shot anyone trying to come near the well to get a drink. We were marched on.

Toward evening, we arrived near a village called Brestowatz where we finally could take a long rest. We were ordered to sit down on the ground. Since there was no place for us to sleep, we slept in the ditch alongside the road in the open. By this time of night the ground had cooled off; and it was quite chilly to sit down on the cold soil. We all huddled together trying to keep warm. We were hungry and thirsty; but we were too tired to eat; and we did not receive any water. We were all freezing terribly because the March nights were still cold; and we had no blankets. Whatever we wore when we left to assemble at the town square was all we had.

In the morning, another day of marching awaited us even though we are all tired and blistered from the previous day's march. It was hard to keep up with the tempo with which the Partisans demanded we march. But whoever could not keep up was shot on the spot. An old man started to stagger and could not keep up. He could not go on without water. The Partisans shot him and wounded him but didn't kill him. When some of the others moved toward him to try to help him, they were shot at in warning to keep away.

We were forced to march on with the man left wounded and dying on the side of the road. I will never forget that scene. No one was allowed to help that poor man. There was no choice – one either marched on or was shot. Children were crying, terrified of the brutal scenes playing out before their eyes. The Partisans showed no mercy. It was another day of horror for both the elderly and the children.

That evening when we arrived in Filipowa, we were again all lined up and all the children ten years old and older were marched away. My twelve-year old brother, Joschi, was among them. As I watched him disappear in the distance, I sobbed with sadness and fear. I didn't know if I would ever see him again. I was six years old and first my father, then my mother, now my only sibling, my beloved brother was taken away.

That night, in Filipowa, again, the ditch next to the road became our bed and we had to sleep in the open all huddled together. It was so terribly cold that night; and we all welcomed the warm sunshine in the morning. That morning we were all split up and the inhabitants of Filipowa were forced to put us up for a few days. What a welcome change. The people were very nice to us and shared their food with us. We finally got water and were even able to wash up. We looked a sight from walking on those dusty roads. Sleeping in comfortable beds again was heavenly.

All in our family were put up in a huge house formerly belonging to a doctor; only the baby sitter, Elfie, was still living in the house. She led us girls into the bedroom of the doctor's wife where we all stayed; and she showed us the tubes of lipstick on the vanity. I never ever had seen a tube of lipstick before so Elfie showed us how to use it. We girls had quite a lot of fun putting makeup all over our faces, looking into the mirror and laughing till our belly hurt.

After we had makeup all over our faces, Elfie played a game with us called "Schuh Wix" (shoe polish). She asked us questions and we had to answer whatever she asked us with the words, "shoe polish." For instance; "What did you eat for supper?" answer: "shoe polish." etc. We thought that a fun game and we laughed and laughed. I can still see little Franzi, doubling up and laughing, when we answered the question of, "What do you brush your teeth with? "Shoe polish!" She temporarily made us forget all the misery we had gone through the past few days.

The reason we were held over in Filipowa was that the entire town of Gakowa, the soon to be "Death Camp," was not ready to house all those people that soon would be confined there. First, all houses had to be emptied of all furniture, belongings, and cattle. All rooms had to be completely bare, only straw covered the floors of every room. All residents of Gakowa fit for work had to be sent to the Labor Camp in Sombor.

Filipowa was also an ethnic German town and they had no idea what was in store for them. After we left, they also were expelled from their homes and taken to the town of Gakowa. But before they were evacuated, however, they had to empty their own houses and take their furniture, their cattle, and their clothing, to designated areas in town and drop them off. Their belongings were then distributed to the Serbs.

That must have been very hard for them to do – getting rid of ones precious belongings and dumping them in a pile on the dirt road. We did not see what happened to our things and it was still hard, knowing that we will never get them back. I remembered my two beautifully dressed porcelain dolls that Mami let me play with when I was sick and wondered what became of them. When their town was emptied of all their belongings, they then also were evacuated, and brought to Gakowa.

After a few days' stay in Filipowa, we were summoned by the drummer to appear at the Filipowa railroad station and were loaded into cattle cars. They really packed us in. It was so crowded that one could not fall over if one fainted - our destination was: "Death Camp Gakowa."

The town of Gakowa in the Province of Batschka was one of the five German speaking towns designated as a major death camp for the annihilation of all ethnic German people in Yugoslavia. The other major death camps were the towns of "Jarek" and "Kruschiwel." "Rudolfsgnad" and "Molidorf" were located in the Province of Banat, Jugoslavia.

Chapter 6
Arrival in Gakowa

When we arrived in Gakowa, we were unloaded and marched into town. The entire town had been emptied of all furniture. Straw covered the floor in every room in every house of the entire town. We were divided into groups and assigned our living quarters. As we came to the first house we were stopped and a group was led into the first room, where straw covered the floor. People were forced to lie down on the floor, one by one, next to each other, like sardines in a can, until the room was filled.

Then another group went to the next room, and so on. People were even assigned to bed down in the cattle stalls, and the barn. This went on all day long until all the people on the train had been assigned a room. We were fortunate that our family was able to be together in the same room although amongst strangers. Sometimes families were split up and children separated from their grandparents. One had no choice. Where they put you, that's where you stayed. There were usually twenty to twenty-five people in a room. Little by little, they brought in people from Filipowa and other nearby German ethnic towns.

Gakowa, a town of three thousand original inhabitants, in a matter of a few weeks housed twenty-one thousand people condemned to die. There was no barbed wire fence to fence us in. There was a living fence of hundreds of Tito's armed Partisan soldiers with bayonet rifles over their shoulders and carrying a pair of binoculars around their neck. They were stationed all around the outskirts of the town, at intervals, and patrolled the outskirts of Gakowa continually, day and night, and shot anyone trying to escape.

That night we got bean soup for supper with a hunk of moldy corn bread. We had to go to a certain house down the street designated as "The Kitchen" and stand in line to receive our meal. There were iron kettles hanging on a tripod that contained the soup. Lisi, Anni, Franzi and I were standing in line and could hardly wait to receive some food. We were all so terribly hungry.

When it was our turn, we received a small metal bowl in which was placed one ladle full of soup. In addition, each of us was handed a piece of moldy cornbread that was as hard as a rock. Then we headed back to our living quarters and sat at the edge of the raised corridor walk-way along the house to eat our soup. One ladle full was all that was allowed per person.

We did not really take a good look at our bowl of soup when it was dished out. We just hurried back quickly because we were so awfully hungry. When we sat down and looked at the contents of the bowl, I could not believe what I saw. I looked at Lisi and said, "There are worms in my soup. I'm not going to eat this. I can't. I won't!" I was disgusted and quickly dumped it.

The bean soup had only a couple of beans in it and some worms and little black bugs floating around in it. There was no salt in it; and it tasted exactly like warm dish washing water. The corn bread was so hard it had to be soaked in the soup in order to be edible. I could NOT eat that soup. We always had good food at home. This looked like pigs slop. This soup looked so bad and seeing the worms and bugs floating in it made my stomach heave.

No one ate anything that night; but the next night, everybody ate it because we were all so terribly hungry. There was nothing else. There were no stores where one could go and buy food. There was no food to be had anywhere in town. It was bean soup and a hunk of rock-hard moldy cornbread only once a day for as long as one was interned in Gakowa.

A good way to eat the soup without throwing up was to not look at what you were eating. First, you dunked the cornbread to get it soggy. Next, you would bring the bowl close to your chin, then either shut your eyes, or stare straight ahead and gobble the soup down as fast as you could. If one tried to eat the cornbread without dunking it, the bread would tear up one's gums and make them bleed. It was like biting into rough sand paper. We did not receive any spoons. When we were done eating, we just went to the well and rinsed out our bowl with cold water and stored it for the next day. We had no soap or hot water to wash out our bowls and no towels to dry them.

Daily, with so little food and moldy corn bread, a lot of people got sick early on. That was Tito's plan. He wanted to starve us to death. He wanted to rid Yugoslavia of all the ethnic German population. It was not uncommon to wake up in the morning and find a dead person lying next to you - which as a child, is just horrifying beyond description.

Periodically, the Partisans came storming into our room and with pointed bayonet guns in hand chased us out into the yard to look us over to see if any children were overlooked that were fit for hard labor. When they saw a child they thought was fit for work, they simply took that child from the grandparents and sent them away to work. I was terrified that I might be taken away from my Grandma, so I would bend my knees under my dress so that I appeared shorter than I was. But all the time my knees were knocking together with fright.

A month after we were placed into the concentration camp, the sound of the drummer again was heard. From past experience, it never meant good news. The drummer's message summoned all to appear at the town square. As we walked along we wondered what it could be this time. Upon coming closer and closer we could hear, from afar, screams of pain from both men and women. Chills went up my spine and I dreaded to think what would happen to us when we got there.

Upon our arrival, we noted wicker baskets lined up; and Partisans searching individuals one by one. Those being searched were removing their jewelry and dropping them each in the proper basket - one for earrings, necklaces, watches, rings, and money. Those reluctant to give up their valuables were brutally beaten. As people were passing on to the new arrivals what was happening ahead of them, some attempted to hide their earrings and other valuables - but where, on such .short notice? I had a pair of tiny gold earrings with a tiny ruby gem that Oma had sown into the hem of my blue wool coat some time ago. Oma sewed Lisi and Anni's earrings also into the hem of their coats.

I had wondered why she did that. Now I understood her foresight. I had forgotten that she had sown them into the side of my bottom hem where it was real bulky. The earrings were a gift from my parents.

I wondered where the Partisans took Mami and Dati. Are they still alive? Daily, I prayed so earnestly for God to keep them all safe. I missed Joschi. I wondered where he was. I longed to see him. I loved my big brother. He always looked out for me.

Waiting in line to be searched was a very stressful scene. People did not want to give up their only possessions they had left. The line crept up closer and closer to those baskets. I was getting nervous. I was hoping they would not find my earrings. I wondered what would happen to me if they found them. My stomach was acting funny; but I could not show my fear although I was shaking in my shoes. My turn came. I was searched from head to toe. I had to remove my shoes for hidden objects. Nothing found in there. Next were my pockets. I was good there. I began to feel uneasy. I held my breath and stood earring less before the Partisan soldier, trembling, as his fingers ran all around my coat sleeves and then inch by inch around my coat hem. My heart was pounding, ready to leap out of my throat. When he reached the end of my bottom hem, he mumbled, "dobro" (good) - words of a satisfactory search and he made the motion to move on to the other side.

Whew! I took a deep breath. A big load lifted off my shoulders. What a sigh of relief! I never attempted to retrieve them for fear of getting seen and having them taken away from me. When the search was over, no one possessed any jewelry or money. It was taken from us and given to the Yugoslavian government – Marshal Tito's Communist regime. I trusted my ear rings were safe where Oma put them.

Periodically a drummer came marching throughout the streets announcing that all people immediately have to line up in front of the house they were staying in. Everyone rushed outside to line up and stood shoulder to shoulder on both sides of the street, waiting.

A few minutes later, we noticed a group of Partisan soldiers in the distance, coming toward us carrying two huge banners and two flags. One banner displayed a picture of Stalin and the other a picture of Tito. The Russian flag was carried ahead of Stalin's banner and the flag of Yugoslavia was carried ahead of Tito's banner. When the Russian and Yugoslav flags came by, we all had to yell, "Schivio Stalin - Schivio Tito." (Interpreted - "long live Stalin- long live Tito). As the flags and two huge banners with a picture each of Stalin and Tito passed by, we had to yell that slogan. Whoever did not yell out was beaten. Seeing the cruel, inhumane treatments that were dealt out to the elderly day by day, them getting beaten, kicked and shot and left to die, and little children dying from starvation, did not warrant praise for Tito. We did not feel like yelling out those slogans because Josip Broz Tito was responsible for ordering mass murders of thousands upon thousands of our people. We were treated worse than animals going to slaughter.

Gakowa, once a nicely, well-kept town of ethnic Germans, was now a town of horror. All the sick, the elderly, the children, and mothers with infants from the whole Province of Batschka were brought here to die. Children had sores all over their body because of severe malnutrition. I was one of them. I was covered from head to toe with sores. They oozed and then formed black scabs the size of a nickel. The oozing sores attracted flies and then became infected. We had no medicine or cream to rub on the sores. They were very painful. It was hard to walk or sit or sleep because the black scabs broke open and bled.

All of us children were mere skin and bones with big distended bellies and hollow eyes, looking pathetic. Our clothes were ragged and dirty after having to wear the same clothes day after day, and not being able to wash them with soap.

Cleanliness was stressed in Sentiwan as we grew up. Girls wore white, bleached petticoats underneath their skirts and now we were humiliated, having to live in this utter filth.

Death was a grim reaper. An average of one hundred people died daily, from starvation, malaria, or typhoid. Huge pits big enough to bury five hundred corpses had to be dug.

When people became sick, they were often too weak to go to the outhouse. They simply soiled the spot where they lay, on the straw covered floor. Since we all slept very near each other, the stench sometimes was overwhelming.

When someone died, the corpse was removed and put outside on the road in front of the house. Sometimes several died in one house and the corpses were stacked up in front of the house like cords of wood. The death wagon went up and down the streets, daily, to collect them.

The corpses were stacked on top of the wagon as many as the wagon could hold; and a young boy walked behind the wagon with his arms up trying to hold on to the corpses to prevent them from falling off. That was the job of boys that were twelve years old and up.

Since there were no coffins in which to bury the dead, no coffin lids concealed the open-mouthed twisted faces and rolled back eyes of the dead. Some of the expressions were very frightening; but this was a day in, day out occurrence. Every day, we children had to pass by a stack of corpses in front of every house when we went to the "Kitchen" to get our soup or wherever we went.

When the bodies of the dead were removed from their spot on the floor, women had the unpleasant task of cleaning the soiled areas. Without soap or disinfectant or rags, the smell was impossible to get rid of. The women would send us kids to find big leaves of weeds (like mullein or comfrey) which were then used to scoop up the mess to be removed. Ashes were then sprinkled on the spots and rubbed in with the leaves, but the odor was never completely gone no matter what was used.

In the summer the odor from the decaying bodies was so bad that it permeated the air throughout the entire town, not only near the cemetery; because there were piles of corpses all throughout town that needed to be picked up and taken to the mass graves.

The mass graves were put behind Gakowa's cemetery because the town's cemetery was already full. Daily, a load of corpses was dropped off at the cemetery. Men from labor camps were brought to Gakowa to dig huge pits to bury the dead. The pits were approximately 20'X 30' and 8' deep.

The corpses were layered on top of another. The men had to walk on top of the corpses to make sure the graves held as many as possible. Mass graves often held five hundred or more corpses. When the pit was full, it was leveled over with dirt and that was that. No one knew where his or her loved ones were buried. We were not allowed to accompany the dead to the grave sight. There were no crosses or name markers allowed on the mass graves.

With 21,000 people now squeezed into a town formerly of 3,000 original inhabitants, the outhouses filled up quickly. Every house in Gakowa usually had one outhouse per family. It was a 4'X4' wooden structure about 7' high with a slanted roof and a door for privacy. It was placed over a hole dug about 5'deep. It had a comfortable seat with a circular hole cut out. Under normal conditions, it usually took a year to fill up before it had to be moved to another area.

With this huge increase in population, people now had no choice but to dig deep ditches with a narrow board to sit on - for the need to "go". We had no lumber to make an enclosure - therefore no privacy. Older people, who could not balance themselves to sit on that narrow board, used the space outside in back of the house when they needed to relieve themselves. That resulted in a huge pile of manure and attracted a lot of flies. The stench was overwhelming, in the summer.

Living in such filth with no soap with which to wash, lice became a huge problem. The straw we were sleeping on became their brooding places. Every morning we would awaken with our clothing and our hair crawling with lice. It brought goose bumps up and down one's spine. Their bites during the night made us itch something awful; and the continual scratching to relieve the itch resulted in big red patches all over our bodies. When a person scratched so hard that it bled, the flies in no time hovered over it and infection set in.

The ongoing activity of the day was to squash lice off each other like monkeys in a zoo. Older people were covered with them more so; because many had lost their eye glasses and had a hard time seeing without them in order to squash them. I remember one incident where I saw an old man sitting on a stump. He was wearing a wool coat with a black velvet collar. The collar was solidly covered with lice; and they were real obvious because the collar was black. As I watched with horror, the lice were crawling from the collar up his neck and into his hair. It made goose bumps go up and down my spine. When someone mentions head lice, that scene flashes before my eyes, even today.

The nightly routine before going to sleep was to take off our undershirt and hunt for the lice. Oma went to the well and drew water into a lawur. When she came in, she sat the big enameled wash bowl on the floor and told us to remove our undershirt, turn it inside out, and shake it over the lawur filled with water, in hopes to dislodge and drown the insects. Next we looked in between the folds of the seam and with both of our thumb nails squashed them. If we neglected to do that, there was no peaceful sleeping that night. We had to do that while it was still day light, since there was no electricity.

Older people who could not kill the lice and went to sleep all covered with them, left way for those critters to roam elsewhere during the night. Therefore, it was a never ending, daily, ongoing activity. When a wound became infected - since we had no medicine -we searched for the weed, "plantain" which has antiseptic qualities. We took several leaves and rubbed them back and forth, between the palms of our hands in order to bruise the leaves and extract juice; and then we placed the bruised leaves with their juice on the wound and it healed.

Because of the unsanitary conditions throughout Gakowa the problem with lice became uncontrollable.

One day a man and a woman came around with clippers to shear the hair off everyone to control the lice. My cousin Lisi and I were running hand in hand when we saw them coming. We did not want to have our hair clipped off. In a split second, I let go of her hand and started to run back to our room to Oma for safety. However, I was not fast enough and they caught me and clipped my hair one strip wide down the center of my head. I was struggling so hard that they could not finish. I managed to get free and ran "home" to Oma. I looked so weird though, that I had to go and let them shear off the rest. Lisi managed to run away and never had hers sheared off. Now everybody was bald; and we could hardly recognize one another - girls looked like boys.

One day in early summer, a group of boys was brought into Gakowa. I recognized my brother, Joschi, among them. In excitement I ran over to him yelling, "Joschi! Joschi!"

I was so happy to see him, I ran to give him a hug. He looked at me with a puzzled expression and asked, "Who are you?"

Since all my hair had been clipped off, he did not recognize me. I could not imagine that he would not be able to recognize his own sister; but we had no mirrors, therefore I didn't know what I looked like. I looked like a boy.

I told him, "I'm your sister." and gave him a hug. I had missed him terribly and I was so happy that he was back with us. He got to stay with us in our room; but he had to work daily in the fields, hoeing corn.

Every day life in Gakowa was the same. The streets were mostly deserted. People stayed in their rooms or the yard of the house they were assigned; because everyone was afraid of the Partisans. One never knew when they would come down the street. Women were usually seen praying.

When we were brought to Gakowa, the elderly of Gakowa, the original inhabitants, did not know themselves what was happening. They did not comprehend the fact that they did not own their house anymore when Tito revoked our citizenship. No one could comprehend that in the twinkle of an eye one lost everything one owned, even when it was completely paid for and debt free. They resented us moving in. They had a hard time with the fact that a lot of strangers were brought into their house.

The owner, an elderly man and his wife, of the house we stayed in, lived in the back room. They had a little granddaughter that lived with them. They had an apple tree in their yard full of apples. They made it known to us that those apples were theirs and told us hands off.

We children yearned so much to have just one apple, but they would not give us any. We were taught by our grandparents to respect the elderly and not steal. When the owners picked their apples and peeled them, they threw out the peels onto the manure pile. Lisi, Franzi, Anni, and I would note when they threw out the peels and then we would go to the manure pile, retrieve them, and eat them. That's how hungry we were.

My cousin Lisi was the first one to get sick with typhoid fever. She was so sick that she could not walk to the outhouse. Both Omas, "Binder" Oma and Lisi and Franzi's Schneider Oma were too weak from malnutrition in order to carry her. A lady named Kowatsch Lisi came from down the street and carried Lisi to the outhouse periodically. I am so glad that she recovered because there were so many that did not make it.

When Lisi got well, we girls used to roam throughout Gakowa and visit different houses to see if we would meet someone from our hometown. The Partisans did not bother children too much if they didn't cause any trouble. We used to sneak into the church building and just sit there for a while. It was so peaceful in there. There was no one else there. Outside all over Gakowa, there was pain, sorrow, filth, stacked up corpses in every street.

Since we only received one bowl of soup per day and one piece of cornbread, we were constantly hungry, looking to find something in nature that we might be able to eat.

In the ethnic German towns all over Yugoslavia the streets were lined with mulberry trees, linden trees, and acacia (honey locust) trees. In the spring we children climbed the acacia trees and picked and ate the blossoms. They tasted real sweet but there were a lot of people that had the same idea. Therefore they were hard to come by. In July the mulberries quickly vanished. Then we also sneaked into the vineyards and ate the grape tendrils, the curly cues that cling as the grape vine grows. They tasted tart.

Then we also kept our eyes to the ground and picked Kaespapple (malva rotundifolia), a low-growing weed called dwarf mallow. It has a seed pod that looks like wheels of cheese. Those tasted good; but the seeds were only the size of a pea. We tried all kinds of weeds that weren't poisonous and ate them; but so did everyone else.

Our Omas once cooked the tops of sugar beets which they had picked in the dark. They tried to convince us that it was spinach. But we were not convinced. We knew what spinach in Sentiwan tasted like. The beet tops tasted horrible. Next they cooked the sugar beets in a tripod kettle and made molasses. They did that way back in the yard while we children were the look-outs to warn them if Partisaner were approaching. I loved the molasses and I believe that I was the only one that did. I was just so awfully hungry all the time, I could almost eat anything. I don't know how in the world they did all of that and were not caught doing it. It was only a one time thing. People went to desperate measures to try to supplement the daily ration of soup. As the months passed, there were no more cats or dogs or weeds to be found in Gakowa. Even sparrows became scarce.

High fever from typhus was raging. The people that had been placed in the cattle stalls and became sick often were found lying in their own excrements; and the stench in there was unbearably nauseating. Bony, lice-covered hands reaching out for help when they sensed someone coming near, reached out in vain - they lay there only to be left unaided and forsaken till death ended their suffering. Those sick and helpless souls were being attacked by the rats at night and often were chewed on. Those that died during the night were found with chunks of flesh eaten away from their bodies by the rats. What possess people to fill their hearts with so much hate that they heap such utter misery upon their fellow man?

Periodically, a group of sick people was brought to Gakowa on a wagon and left to die because they were too sick to work. They were brought here generally from various forced labor camps – Sombor, Esseg, or Besdan and others. Anyone that became seriously ill on a job, without hope of getting better was sent to Gakowa to die.

Our mothers and fathers were treated like slaves. The head Labor Camp was located in Sombor. From there, laborers were sent to various places for work duties. Any Serb or Hungarian citizen needing hired help could come to the Labor Camp and buy a laborer for a day or a month or however long needed for a very cheap price. After they were no longer needed, they then would have to return the hired help to the Labor Camp; and again that person was resold for new work duties and a new price.

When a wagon full of sick people was brought into Gakowo, the children who had no grandparents would run over to the wagon to check, if perhaps, their moms or dads might be on the wagon. I sometimes went along with the group of children. We would play with each other daily, trying to forget the misery of Gakowa. When we spotted a Partisan soldier coming down the street, we would simply go into the house nearby and hide.

When the orphans asked the sick on the wagon that were brought in that day, if they knew the whereabouts of their parents and they did not; then the children walked away broken hearted. Although I did not know the whereabouts of my own mother and father, I still had my grandparents. I tried to make the children feel better, so we all went to a place by ourselves and I told them my favorite fairy tales; Rapunzl, Rumpelstilzchen, Red Riding Hood, Dornroeschen, etc. that my Knoebl Oma used to tell me before she died of cancer. It used to lift their spirits and those tales made us all feel better.

One day in early summer, I spotted my father on the "sick wagon" among the people who were brought into Gakowa that day. My heart sank when I saw him looking so pale and weak; but I was happy to see him. He was very sick - near death. I ran over to him, but all he could say when he saw me was, "Mei Kindi!" (my child). I could smell the odor from the infection in his lungs when he spoke and he spit up blood when he coughed. He had pneumonia to the point of death and was placed in the house across the street from the house we stayed in.

There was an old lady in her eighties named Heger Res-Besl, (Bas or Besl means aunt and Res is short for Theresa) an original inhabitant of Gakowa, who took it upon herself to take care of him. The old lady made him a bed of straw in an open porch that was spun over with a vine of blooming flowers. She said he needed fresh air to get better. Res-Besl went and brought him his soup and moldy cornbread and fed him and cared for him. He was struggling with life and death for six weeks.

I was so worried about him. I constantly went over there to see if there was any sign of improvement. Every time I went, he was still the same, unresponsive. I missed talking to him. I would get this heavy feeling in my chest and tears welled up in mine eyes when I looked at him laying there so sick. I wanted him to feel better.

Checking on his condition daily with no improvement seemed unbearably long. Daily, streams of prayers were sent to heaven above. Oma not feeling well herself, did her best to help Res Besl take care of him. Oma was at his side night and day and helped to change his clothes and rinse them out. Because of his high fever, he sweated profusely and his clothes were constantly soaked with perspiration. There was no soap to be had. There was no doctor to check him. There was no medicine for the sick. She made tea from Linden blossoms, sage leaves, mullein, and chamomile blossoms to extract healing properties and gave it to him to drink.

Next door to Res- Besl lived a Serbian lady who was given the house she lived in by the state of Yugoslavia because her husband, a Partisan soldier, was killed in the war. (The house originally belonged to a German family but it was confiscated and given to her because Tito had nullified the citizenship of ethnic Germans.) She was a kind lady and brought Dati a glass of milk every day because she owned a cow; and she felt sorry for him. Occasionally, she brought him an apple and a bunch of grapes.

One should never hate and judge a group of people for who they are just because a few are hateful. I prayed earnestly for Dati to get well. I also prayed that God would keep Mami safe and hopefully someday we'd all be united again.

Little by little Dati improved. Eventually he recovered completely.

Chapter 7
Dati is Well Again

After Dati got well, he had to work in the Wagon Repair Shop. His job was repairing wagons that were used to haul the food supplies from the city of Sombor. His other job was to chop wood and make kindling for the cooking of the soup for the entire town. Tettman Stefan Vetter, Dati's former business partner and Dati were both responsible for chopping the wood needed for cooking the soup. Dati also made wooden sandals for the cooks in the kitchen. Dati was very skilled in wood working.

While he was in the work shop, he decided to make a gift for Commandant Schutzo, the man in charge of the Death Camp. He was a young, skinny man in his twenties, very arrogant, who was feared by everyone. Observing all the dead piled up at the cemetery brought a smile on his bony face. He was capable of bringing everyone to his knees.

Dati made a small wine barrel as a gift because he knew Schutzo loved to drink and entertain his soldiers. This gift would be unique because it was a table-top version that would hold both red and white wine without the two colors getting mixed up. The trick was in the spigot. Dadi was hoping to impress Schutzo and win the favor of the Commandant and maybe get permission to fetch supplies from the Labor Camp in Sombor. Maybe he would then be able to learn of the welfare of Mami who used to work in the labor camp in Sombor.

When Dati presented his gift to Schutzo and showed him how it worked, Schutzo was greatly impressed and considered him as a comrade (friend). Dati's intentions were not to buddy up with him. He had something else in mind.

A few weeks later, Schutzo summoned Dati and asked him: "Henrich, could you make another barrel? I want to give one to my comrade?" Dadi said: "Surely, I would, but I don't have all the supplies on hand needed to make one. I need the metal bands that hold the barrel together." To this Schutzo replied, "I'll give you a Tosvoy (a pass) and then you can get the supplies you need to make another one.

Dati had accomplished what he had hoped for by making this gift. He wanted to find out where Mami was. The last time he saw her, he got a glimpse of her washing windows in the hospital in Sombor. The only way that he could go to Sombor was to get the supplies for the barrel himself. The Partisans did not know what he needed. By going himself, he could stop at the Labor Camp and maybe find out where she was and her welfare.

Dati could speak the Serbian language very well and he loved to joke around with people. Often when he joked around with the Partisans, he was able to get all kinds of information from them without them knowing it.

One day in late summer when the corn began to form big ears and the husks had turned brown, a group of us girls decided to sneak into the corn field on hands and knees and snitch us each an ear of cattle corn. We then pulled back the dried husks and shredded it finely with our fingers and braided the husks into "hair" and pretended it to be our doll. After each of us had our "doll," we decided to head for "home."

As I raised my eyes to check out if the coast was clear of any soldier, I caught hold of a very familiar figure. I rubbed my eyes to make sure I really saw what I saw. Sure enough, it was Mami limping through the corn. I ran toward her and hugged her and just hugged her. We sneaked back to the house where we were placed when we came to Gakowa.

After we arrived in our room, Mami told me that she had come from the Labor Camp in Sombor. That was where they took them when they were marched out of Sentiwan. Her job was to cook the pea soup for those returning nightly from their forced labor duties. She was in the kitchen and they ran out of water. It was always her duty to fetch water; so she picked up the big water can and headed for the well which was just outside the barbed-wire fence surrounding the compound. When she came to the gate near the well, there was no soldier guarding the gate, nor any Partisan soldier to be seen in the entire yard. At a split second she decided to make a run for it and managed to sneak out without being seen. Someone had mentioned once that the railroad tracks in Sombor go straight to Gakowa and she decided to try it. She walked all night long in the dark and did not know for sure where she would end up. It is an eighteen kilometer walk. That is far if one does not know for sure if it's the right way. She was tired.

Oh how good it was to see Mami again. She was able to sneak in without being detected. No one knew she was here except the people that occupied the room with us. Oma at this time was very sick and could no longer walk or even talk. Mami was shocked when she saw her lying there so awfully sick. She lay listless on her bed of straw on the floor. Oma's whole body was covered with lice. No matter how much we tried to squash them, we could not keep them off. It made me very sad. We knew death was waiting at the door. I forced myself not to think about Oma going to die. I did not want to face the fact. I refused to think about it. Mami was sad to see Oma so very sick.

I held on to Mami's hand and did not let go of her. I asked her many, many questions. It did not seem real that she was actually here. Then Joschi came walking into the room after his field work was done. She saw her first born standing before her. Mami's eyes lit up. She limped to him and embraced him and hugged him. Words flowed from her lips, "Gott sei Dank! You're alive." Tears rolled down her cheeks. She cried so hard her whole body trembled. She had worried herself sick for six months, not knowing if any of us were alive or not, or of our whereabouts.

When Dati came back from his work duty, he could not believe that Mami was standing in our room. He ran to her and hugged and kissed her. They just stood there in embrace. We all cried. They were happy tears. Some people in the room thought it foolish for her to try to sneak into the Death Camp when everyone in here tried to find a way out. We had had no knowledge of her whereabouts either.

Mami's explanation for coming here was because of a rumor she had heard that Dati was in Gakowa on the verge of death. She had heard so many horror stories about Gakowa that she absolutely had to know how we all were doing. She could not bear the "not knowing."

That night it was so nice to snuggle up to Mami when we went to sleep on our bed of straw, on the floor. All four of us were back together again. My last thoughts were "Thank you God!" Then I fell asleep.

In the morning, Dati and Joschi had to go to their work assignments. Nobody knew that Mami had sneaked into Gakowa. Since the Partisans didn't know she was here she stayed in the room so she wouldn't get into trouble. When she woke up she had a very sore foot. Her heel had become infected and had a big lump on it, the size of an egg. It was extremely hard for her to walk. She had walked eighteen kilometers from Sombor to Gakowa without shoes. No wonder.

I was so happy she was here with us. I had my Mami back again. I had her all to myself and I did not leave her side all morning. We just talked and talked. There were so many questions that needed an answer. We all found out that Mami and all the people in the Labor Camp in Sombor and we in Gakowa, all were given only one ladle of soup per day. There was never any breakfast or any lunch served all the while we lived here. We talked non-stop until noon.

All of a sudden two Partisan soldiers with bayonet rifles came storming into our room. They walked toward Mami and said, "Get up, Lisa; you're going back to Sombor. Commandant Rajko wants you back immediately. You had no permission to come here. Let's go!" (They knew Mami well because she did Commandant Rajko's laundry at the Labor Camp in Sombor.)

I held on to Mami's hand and cried, "Mami... No... they can't do that. You just got here. You can't walk back to

Sombor with your sore foot." They grabbed me and pulled me away from her. I screamed, "NO....NO...NO!"

Mami told me to hush. She had no choice. If she didn't go with them, they would shoot her. I did not want them to shoot her so I backed off. Sadness swept over me. I was sobbing. I could not bear to see her leave. Mami gave me a hug and a kiss and said, "Gott behiet dich!" (God keep you safe) and limped toward them, ready to go. Just before they stepped out the door, Mami stopped and asked them, "Please just grant me one request. Let me say good-bye to my dying Mother-in-law, there on the floor."

They nodded their heads. Mami walked over to the spot where Oma lay and knelt down next to her. As I watched, Mami tenderly took hold of Oma's hand and placed it in hers and stroked her gently and said, "I guess this is the last time we'll ever see each other. God bless!" Tears started to run down Mami's face and mine followed. As Mami held Oma's hand in hers, the lice started crawling from Oma's hands onto Mami's hands. The scene was just so unbearably sad – Oma about to die and Mami having to leave.

I quietly sobbed as they led Mami out the door. I felt as though my heart was tearing in pieces. Tears rolled down my cheeks. I did not want to cause a scene. I did not want Mami to get into trouble and get shot.

I followed behind them out the door, out the gate, and then I leaned against the fence and stared down the street. Mine eyes followed them. As I stood there, questions raced through my mind, "What will they do with Mami when she gets back to Sombor? Will they beat her? Will they shoot her? Oh, Mami, Mami, Mami! I can't bear to be without you again. I'll be all alone when Dati and Joschi have to go to work. Please, please, please, **PLEASE! DEAR GOD!** Please don't let them shoot her." I watched them lead her away, Mami limping badly, a soldier on each side. I stared into the distance till I could see them no more; and then I just stood there, alone, sobbing.

When Dati walked into our room that night, I ran over to him crying, "Two Partisans came and took Mami back to Sombor. What will they do to her? Will they punish her? We will never know."

Dati knew that the soldiers took her back; because the Partisans came to the work shop and asked him where Lisa was and informed him that she had to go back to Sombor because Commandant Rajko demanded it.

Dati immediately went to Commandant Schutzo and said, "Forgive my insolence; but my wife escaped from Sombor to see about my welfare since I was very sick. I implore you. Is there no way that you could intervene and get Commandant Rajko's permission to have her stay in Gakowa? She can work here too?"

Schutzo replied, "Henrich, there is no way! Rajko wants her back and that's that. No more discussion. Go back to your work! Tito's law is that families have to be split up. Those able to work are put to work as slaves without pay and the elderly and children are doomed for annihilation. Husbands and wives are not allowed to be together in the same camp."

The Partisans took Mami back to Sombor using the train; because she could hardly walk when she left.

Chapter 8
Typhoid Out of Control

Typhoid fever became rampant. My cousin, little Franzi, also came down with it. He had a very high fever and kept babbling all kinds of nonsense, hands and feet were constantly moving. He and I used to play with each other a lot before he got sick. We made many mud pies together. I missed him very much. All day long, every day, I constantly went to check to see if perhaps, there was just a tiny bit of improvement, but all he did was babble nonsense every time I went to see him. His hands and feet were real fidgety. He was very ill and it took a long time for him to get better.

Franzi's mother, my aunt Rosl-Bas and her sister, Noni, had been sent from the Labor Camp in Sombor to work in our hometown, Sentiwan. When Rosl-Bas heard that Franzi had typhoid, she and her sister, Horn Noni-Bas, sneaked from Sentiwan into Gakowa to take care of him because Oma was already too weak from starvation. I was so glad that they were here. Rosl-Bas cared for Franzi and Noni-Bas (Aunt Anna) looked after Oma.

When people were sent to work in certain places, they sent them in groups. They did not keep records of laborers because the Partisans did not know how to write. When someone was missing on their work detail, there was no way to trace their whereabouts. Because they often shot people at an instant without warning if one did not quickly obey, it was no big deal to the Partisans if people were missing.

Because typhoid was so contagious, those who contracted it were separated from the others and were put in special houses. Even the Partisans feared coming down with it. We children would go to these houses to check to see who was still alive. There was no one to tell us that we shouldn't do that. Everyone around us was sick and we just wandered throughout town to check on people.

One day I went to see about my aunt Knoebl. She had contracted typhoid fever and was put in this special house for those ill with it. Watching the sick with typhoid was horrible to see. She died and left two children orphaned, my cousins, Knoebl, Leni and little Andres. To this day, I can't get it out of my mind, watching the lice crawling in and around the sick peoples' eyes; and lice crawling up and down peoples arms as they lay there helpless; and lice crawling all over their head and in and out of their ears and down their neck. It made my skin crawl. Seeing people in this condition is something you will never ever forget.

With typhus raging and people dying from starvation, there was no more room at the cemetery for new graves. So by the end of September 1945, mass graves had to be dug behind the cemetery. The daily death toll kept increasing. After Mami was taken back to Sombor, Oma's condition worsened day by day. I could not bear the thought that she would soon be gone also.

I remembered how hard it was for me to watch when Oma Knoebl passed away from cancer – her body wracked with pain when I went to see her every day.

I did not want the same for Oma now. But I did not want to let her go. I struggled daily with that thought. I prayed so hard for her; but I knew the conditions in Gakowa were just too horrible.

Oma died from starvation October 7, 1945. I was so devastated by her death that I completely blocked it out of my memory. My brother helped put Oma's corpse on the death wagon and it was taken to the sight of the mass graves.

Because I could not talk about Oma's death, Dati told me months later that he went to the sight of the mass graves where the corpses were dropped off. He removed Oma's corpse from the death wagon and put it on a wheelbarrow and pushed her to the cemetery, dug a hole, and buried her in a grave for her alone. He did not want his mother to be just thrown into a mass grave. That was real hard and sad for Dati to do. He did that at night after his work duty. There were so many men digging in the area of the mass graves that he did not look suspicious doing what he did.

I found out later why Omas were the first to die. They often gave up their food to their grandchildren.

Ten days later my Opa also died. I remember waking up one morning and seeing my Opa, cold and stiff. He had died during the night. Opa used to send me to fetch mullein leaves so that he could wrap up his legs with them because he had sores on his legs. He used them as bandages. My Urendl, Knoebl Regina (my great grandma) also died in October from starvation. The elderly were so skinny and weak that they resembled mere skin covered skeletons staggering around.

After Oma had died, my brother and I moved in where Dati stayed, across the street. Noni-Bas, (Aunt Anna) my father's oldest sister, came and lived with us also.

Daily, Joschi had to work in the corn fields. One day when Joschi came home after working in the fields, he went to hang around with his friends. Sometime later on, he came into our room with a smile on his face holding a dead sparrow. He told Noni-Bas that he wanted his sister to have it when it was cooked. Noni-Bas gutted the sparrow, plucked its feathers and cooked it.

He had taken a sling shot and shot the sparrow for his sister to eat. The piece of meat after it was cooked was the size of a walnut. He should have eaten it because he shot it; but he gave it up for me. I have never forgotten it. I love my brother. He was the best brother any girl growing up could ever have had.

Many people, (mostly old men) who could not deal with those horrible conditions in the camp and saw no hope of ever getting free, hanged themselves, leaving their loved ones alone and in despair. News of bad events like those were quickly spread by us kids who wandered throughout town. Many tried to escape; but very few made it. Those who attempted it, paid with their lives.

A friend of my father and his daughter, who was my good friend and playmate, attempted to escape one night. They were caught and thrown into the prison cellar, where they were kept for a few days. This cellar was used as a jail cell for those who had been caught, trying to escape. The captives were escorted to the outhouse only twice a day.

The stench coming from that cellar when the trap door was opened was overwhelming. They were kept there in the dark cellar for a few days. Then my friend and her dad were pulled out and taken into the street. The Partisans then decided to make an example of them, to show everyone what would happen if caught. The Partisans took a pitchfork and stabbed them over and over and over again - and they died. I was shocked! What a horrible death. That was my dear friend, Leni. What inhumane treatment! From that experience, I secretly hoped that my father would **never try to escape** from Gakowa.

Wanting to share my grief with my cousin Lisi, I went across the street to see her, only to find out that she was gone. No one knew what happened to her. In fact everyone of her family was gone – her Schneider Oma and Anni. There was no explanation. That was life in Gakowa. I walked sadly across the street, went into our room and sobbed. Noni'Bas was gone. I could not find her anywhere. Everyone I loved was gone. I missed Lisi. I missed little Franzi. I missed Anni. I felt so alone. It seemed forever until Dati and Joschi walked into our room that night. Oh how glad I was to see them both walking through the door.

Chapter 9
The Bitter Winter of 1945-1946

Fall came and went. The temperature began to drop and it became uncomfortably cold in our room. We had no heat. There was no heat in any of the houses in Gakowa where ethnic Germans were confined, except in the building of the former city hall of Gakowa. It became the Partisans' headquarters that now housed Schutzo, the Camp Commander. The houses surrounding the city hall were chosen for the living quarters for the Partisan soldiers. They were also heated and kept warm.

The internees were not provided with any wood to heat the living quarters all winter long. People scrounged around trying to gather twigs and branches and scrap lumber to make a fire in the Dutch tile ovens in the rooms. Even dry cornstalks were gathered from the fields and burned; but those burned up real fast and were gone in a flash.

The winter of 1945 had arrived. It was one of the coldest winters on record, with deep snow. In the stillness of the night I could hear the wind howling and cold air began seeping through the window frames and underneath the door penetrating every inch of the room. It seemed that death was reaching in with her fingers trying to claim the elderly and babies. Many elderly, small children, and babies froze to death during the nights. Between one hundred and one hundred twenty corpses were collected daily.

It was the worst winter that I have ever experienced. It was so very cold, so bone-chillingly cold. People became desperate and started to tear off the window frames and the inside door frames and hacked up inside doors and burned them; but that did not go very far. The winter was too long.

My fingers and toes were numb and we all tried to huddle together to keep warm and rubbed each others arms and legs to get circulation going. It was hard going to sleep with the constant shivering. Oh how I wished to be able to crawl under a down comforter that we used to have back home in Sentiwan to cover with in winter or to be able to sit near a ceramic tile hearth and feel the gentle heat radiating throughout the room.

I snuggled up to Dati and then I pulled up my knees to my chest and pulled my blue wool coat over my legs as a blanket. So many people froze to death during the night as time went by. It was scary to think about it. I did not want to freeze to death. I did not want to be thrown on top of all those frozen corpses on the death wagon and be dumped into a big hole. I was terrified to go to sleep. "Please God; don't let me freeze to death. I want to live. I want to see Mami again. Please don't let me die."

All of a sudden with a big blow, the door was knocked open. Cold air rushed into the room. Two Partisan soldiers with rifle in hand came toward me and pulled me up by my arms and dragged me outside. They marched me, only me, to the cemetery to an already dug-open grave. They put me into the hole, both pointing the rifle at me. One was standing behind me. The other one was facing me.

They both had this big smirk on their faces showing what a pleasure it was for them to kill me. They put their finger on the trigger. I begged them not to kill me. They just laughed and laughed. I tried to scream for help; but no sound came out of my mouth. I tried and tried but could not scream.

I thought this was the end. I took my hands and covered mine eyes. I heard a click. I screamed as loud as I could. I suddenly sat up with sweat on my forehead.

It was dark. I felt Dati's hands around me and his voice whispering, "It's only a dream. Don't be afraid. It's only a dream. Everything's all right. He tried to assure me. I was shaking. He held me even tighter and suggested I try to sleep. In the morning when I awoke, I was so relieved. I was not shot to death. I did not freeze to death. "Our Father in heaven -Thank you!"

For years, I was reluctant to go to sleep at night for fear of getting another nightmare. I had the same dream periodically over and over until I was thirteen years old.

Snowflakes began dancing from the sky and little by little covered up the piles of manure found in every yard of every house in town and turned everything into a magical glistening white. It reminded me of Christmas; but there would be no Christmas for us this year. We had no calendar; and therefore, we had no inkling as to what month or day it was. Besides, we were not even aloud to sing. There was just misery, hunger, death, and cold.

Oh how I missed Oma! If she were alive, I could snuggle up to her. Dadi was mostly gone working and getting supplies for the Commandant and his men. On one of those trips, he ran into Mami in the kitchen at the Labor

Camp in Sombor; and when he came home, he had good news. Mami was alive! I was so relieved to find out that Mami was alive - that she was alright. They didn't shoot her. "Gott sei Dank!" -"Thank you, our God!"

That news was better than any Christmas present I could have received if we could have celebrated Christmas. Oh, how I longed to be surrounded by Mami's arms. I remember back home when I used to play outside in winter and came in with ice cold hands, Mami used to say, "Come here and put your hands under my arms," and in no time my hands were warm as toast.

As I gazed out the window one evening, I noticed the moon shining brightly on the new fallen snow making everything glisten and sparkle. It looked so magical - everything white and clean. As I stood there in amazement I momentarily forgot where I was and began reminiscing of times past back at home in Sentiwan at Christmas time.

Back home, Christmas season started Dec. 6, when all the children in town placed their shoes outside next to the door before going to bed at night, in hopes that Nickolaus (Santa Claus) would stuff them with goodies while they were sleeping. If we had been good, then we would find candy, oranges, and chocolate stuffed in them in the morning. If we had been bad, then they were found empty.

After "Nickolaus" day had passed, mothers and grandmothers would get busy and start baking Honig Bakatscheln (Honey Cookies) so that they could rest and become soft and be just right by Christmas.

I loved to help. First, Mami rolled out a long piece of dough like a long sausage and then cut it every inch or so. Then we would flour our hands because the dough was very sticky and roll them into balls and place them on the cookie sheet, and in the oven they went. They were carefully baked and when cooled were all dumped into a big bowl containing powdered sugar and egg white icing. They were then stirred so every part was covered with the white icing and then laid out to dry overnight. Then the cookies were stored for a couple of weeks in a tin.

A week before Christmas, Puepple (Pipple) were made. I used to love to cut out angels, and stars and bells and paint them with beaten egg whites and sprinkled them with granular sugar on top and baked them. We had no food coloring then. I hoped for a misshapen one that came out a little crooked; and Mami used to let me eat it to see if it tasted alright. Mag Strudl (poppy seed strudl) and Nuss Strudl (Walnut Strudl) were also baked. It was a joyous time and a time for the best eating all year.

While we were waiting for Christmas Eve to come, Oma would tell us that on Christmas Eve, as soon as it got dark, Kristkindl (The Christ Child) would come down from heaven on a long ladder and bring goodies for children that have been good.

If we were bad, however, Kristkindl would bring along Knecht Ruprecht. He was a big strong grumpy man who rounded up bad children and hauled them away in a big burlap sack. He wore a big Bunda, (a long brown, shearling lamb-skin rug) that was draped over him, hanging way down to the floor. He had a chain and a switch and he would hit the bad kids with the switch and tie them up with the chain and drag them away.

When Christmas Eve arrived and it began to get dark, butterflies started to stir in my stomach with excitement and anticipation on waiting and wondering - would Kristkindl come with goodies or could I be dragged away by Knecht Ruprecht, had I, sometime, been naughty?"

At the sound of a tiny tinkle of a bell and a knock at the door, Kristkindl would enter with a small Christmas tree and Knecht Ruprecht and ask the question: "Have you been good?"

If a child had misbehaved during the year, it would get switched a few times and asked: "Do you promise to be good?" If one didn't promise, then Knecht Ruprecht would attempt to take you along. So every child promised to be good out of fear.

Next, Kristkindl would set the tree down and then asked: "Can you sing and pray?" We would answer: "Yes!" Then we sang Stille Nacht (Silent Night) and I sang to the best of my abilities. While looking at them both with amazement and fear, Knecht Ruprecht looked so fearful with his deep voice and holding a switch and a chain and a big sack. I made a vow within me to be good next year so I would not get dragged away with him. Then I looked on with awe at Kristkindl all dressed in a long white beautiful dress and a white veil over the head and carrying a bag of gifts.

When we were done singing and giving our promise to be good, Kristkindl reached into the bag and brought out a small bowl, full of beautifully wrapped hard candy, and poured it out onto the floor. Then we scampered to pick it up and gather up all we could. Then Kristkindl reached in again and brought forth the most beautiful big oranges that I was hoping to get and yearned for all year long and also brought forth a wreath of dried figs and a bag of chestnuts.

After we promised to be good and said, "Danke Schoen!" (Thank you very much"), Kristkindl left with Knecht Ruprecht. When they were gone, we set up the tree and decorated it with a few beautiful glass blown ornaments of pine cones, balls, and colorful glass birds. Then we would clip on candle holders at the very tips of the branches and place the candles in them. After it was all decorated, Mami would light the candles and we all sat around the tree and sang our favorite Christmas songs: O Tannenbaun, Leise rieselt der Schnee, O du Froehliche, etc. When we were done singing, the candles were blown out and we started sampling the gifts we received. It was a magical night.

Then I remembered all the fun we had when New Year's Eve arrived. Dati and Mami would tell us New Year's Eve, that whoever was the first one to wish them "Happy New Year!" on New Year's morning would receive a silver coin. That made me want to go to bed early to make sure I'd be the first to get up. I wanted that silver coin. On New Year's Day, already at 5:00 a.m., - after we were done wishing Dati and Mami and received our first coin - we kids were ready to go wishing. We'd walk in groups, in the dark and headed toward Oma and Opa's room first, then on to Urendl's (great-grandma's.) Next, we proceeded to visit aunts and uncles, friends and neighbors. We recited the same wish everywhere we went in the "Danube Swabian dialect:

> "Ich winsch Eich a glickseliches Neies Jahr!
> lang'es Lewe, G'sundheit, Fried un Einichkeit,
> un die ewich Glickselichkeit!"

Translated: "I wish you a blissful Happy New Year! Long life, good health, peace, unity, and eternal blissful happiness!"

Everyone received us with gladness; and after reciting our greeting, rewarded us with cookies and some coins. It was a fun time because everyone we wished, "Happy New Year!" gave us some good things to eat and some coins. At the end of the day, we would wind up with a nice little sack of coins.

The whole day was spent visiting and enjoying our time with family and friends and eating good food.

Chapter 10
My First Escape

Then very early one morning, I felt a tap on my shoulder and I knew immediately what that meant. The night before, Dati had told me in secret: "Kindi, tomorrow morning, very early, while it is still dark, I will take you to see Mami in Sombor." Hearing those words brought such excitement that I could hardly control myself, to keep from screaming. I could not share my joy with anyone else in the room. I was so elated that blood rushed immediately throughout my veins, and the terrible feeling of being cold temporarily left me. "Oh! To see Mami again!" whirled through my mind.

I could not go to sleep for a long time - if morning were only here. Any fear of getting caught magically left me. I finally fell asleep after toying with my thoughts for hours.

I could feel Dati's hands reach for my hand and I immediately knew what that meant. I instantly rose to my feet and followed, tip-toeing very carefully so not to accidentally step on someone sleeping and awaken them. I was already dressed because we had no blankets and I had to sleep every night fully dressed in shoes, stockings, dress, and my blue wool coat.

When Dati opened the door and we stepped outside, windy, ice cold air hit me in the face and surrounded us;

and immediately goose bumps crawled all over my body. The snow was ankle deep; and Dati scooped me up so I would not get my feet all wet. I could hear the whinny of the horses as he carried me to the wagon awaiting us on the street in front of the gate of the house. I put my arms around Dati's neck and held on tight. I was so happy to have my Dati all well and my thought rose to heaven, "Thank You God!" I was so happy. The horses whimpered as Dati put me on the wagon.

He proceeded to take one of the Bundas (brown sheep skin rug) that was draped over the hard wooden bench that he was sitting on and wrapped me snuggly into it and put me underneath the bench. With a whisper, he strongly admonished me not to talk until we were at our destination. He did not want to take a chance of someone hearing me talk at the wrong moment and ruin his plan.

Then he carefully draped the other Bunda over the bench so that anything under it was out of sight. He took hold of the reins and with two clicks of his tongue to signal the horses to start up, we started sleighing along.

My emotions were both full of fear and excitement – fearful, because we had to go past the guard stationed at the exit of Gakowa and the chance of me being found, if the wagon was searched, and thrown into that horrible dark cellar - joyful, of the hope of soon being again with Mami. My emotions switched back and forth from fear to joy.

It seemed like an eternity until we reached the place where Dati had to stop to show his pass and get the OK from the guard to leave Gakowa.

Then I heard Dati yell: "Whoa!" At that moment my heart began to pound and I knew instantly that I had to be very still. I hoped that I would not have to cough or sneeze. I immediately directed my thoughts to heaven and pleaded with God for help.

Dati greeted the guard saying, "Dobro Judro!" (Good Morning) and showed him his Tosvoj (permission pass) and then I heard the guard say: "Dobro!" (Good) and he motioned Dati to go on. Again I heard the sound of two clicks of Dati's tongue to start up the horses and I knew we were safe. "Thank You God!" we're safe.

It was 18 Km from Gakowa to Sombor and the wagon just slid along. I remembered Dati's admonition: "No talking till we're there!" Although I had my knees drawn up to my chest and lay there in a cramped position, for the first time all winter long I felt toasty warm. What a good feeling. I was like a bug, snug in a rug (I was wrapped up in a sheepskin rug called Bunda). I had a worry free feeling. God's never failing care surrounded me. All I could think of was Mami. I had not seen her since last September when she had escaped from Sombor and after one day was summoned back. I was so glad that they didn't shoot her. I thanked God for watching over us and I could hardly wait to get there. After a long time, I don't know how long, I could hear the clip clop sounds the horses hoofs made walking on the stone street; and I also heard the sounds of other horse-drawn wagons passing us. I knew it would not be long - we were in Sombor.

Soon thereafter I heard Dati's voice, "Whoa!" and the wagon came to a stop. My heart raced. Dadi lifted the Bunda that was draped over the bench and reached for my hand. I took hold of his hand and he pulled me out from under the bench and un-wrapped me. He then jumped off the wagon and held out his arms and I jumped; and he carried me to the back door of the house.

With a knock, the door opened wide and there stood a short, older lady, a little rounded, very friendly, with dark hair and brown eyes, greeting us and inviting us in. We hurriedly stepped inside and shut the door. "I'm Mrs. Bartlitsch and you must be Lisl," she said. "We've been waiting to meet you. We got up very early this morning so that we would have everything ready when you got here."

Mine eyes searched for Mami. She immediately could tell and said, "She will be here soon. She went to the cellar to get things for breakfast." We entered the kitchen and the warmth immediately surrounded me. It was a large, nicely furnished room with a big table, cooking hearth, china cabinet, a water pump at the kitchen sink, and even a day bed in one corner. After having lived in Gakowa a full year with no furniture in any of the rooms, only straw on the floor, it was hard for my eyes to absorb and get a good glimpse of a truly furnished room after such a long time.

Then suddenly Mami stepped into the kitchen with her arms full, carrying bread and milk and butter. She hurriedly put down the items. Seeing Mami with arms wide open, I flew into her arms and planted a slew of kisses all over her face and we hugged and hugged and hugged. Dati stood there with a relaxed and pleasing look on his face. What joy, what happiness! "Oh, Mami! I missed you SO much!"

Mrs. Bartlitsch asked Dati to sit down for a moment to have some warm milk and bread and butter before he headed out; because he had to get his supplies and was expected back in Gakowa. He could not afford to have the Partisans suspect what he had been up to.

After he finished eating, we exchanged lots of hugs and kissed and he left. I was not afraid for him. I knew he'd be all right. The Partisans would not hurt him. They had a lot of respect for him. My dad had always been very pleasant to everyone in authority and never gave anyone any suspicion. He conducted himself always honorably and planned things out very carefully. They had no clue that Dati smuggled me out. They did not keep records of people because most Partisans did not know how to read or write.

After Dadi got his supplies, he headed back to Gakowa to deliver them to Schutzo's headquarters and after his daily work at the Wagon Repair shop he went "home" to be with my brother. So it was now just the two of them from our family, living in Gakowa. Everyone related to us had died.

After Dati had gone, Mrs. Bartlitsch went to get Mr. Bartlitsch who ran a grocery store in the front part of their house and was organizing items before the store opened. A man in his early 50's entered, of medium height about 5'10" a good natured man and on the slim side. He was pleasant but not overly friendly like his wife.

I was introduced and I was told that I could stay at their house with Mami; but that nobody must know that I was living there. If someone happened to come visit them, then I had to hide under the bed and stay there till they were gone.

For breakfast, I was served hot milk and bread with butter on it. It tasted so good. What a difference compared to the moldy cornbread in Gakowa. After I finished eating, I was given a bath and had my hair shampooed and was deloused and Mami washed my clothes and my wool coat was taken to the dry cleaner.

It was such a good feeling to be clean all over- to be washed with soap and to wear clean clothes. For the first time after 11 months I slept in a real bed again with sheets and a warm down comforter and with Mami. I was happy.

The Bartlitsch family was a real nice Croatian family. They owned and operated a grocery store in Sombor about two kilometers from the Head Labor Camp. By discovering that hired help was to be had real cheap from the Labor Camp, they went and employed my mother as their housekeeper since running a store kept them both real busy. After finding out about my mother's life and her children in the Death Camp, they decided to chance it to harbor me in their house if Dati could smuggle me out of Gakowa. I could stay at their house as long as Mami worked there.

It was sometime in March 1946, when I arrived at their house and I stayed there one month until the slaughter of an ethnic German man, a prisoner at the Labor Camp.

The Bartlitsches were very nice people and Mami and I got to eat our meals with them. They had a daughter named Irene, a tall beautiful girl in her mid twenties with beautiful shiny black hair and dark brown eyes. She was very nice to me and put in a lot of effort to teach me proper etiquette.

My first lesson was to eat canned Black Cherries, like a little lady should. After having lived in Gakowa for one year, I just gobbled food down as fast as I could; because I was always so terribly hungry. Irene tried to slow my eating habits down a bit. At their table I could eat all I wanted without fear of anyone taking it away from me.

Irene put a cup full of cherries into a bowl and gave me a tea spoon. I had to sit up straight with mouth over the bowl. Then I had to take my spoon and place one cherry at a time and put it in my mouth, eat the meat off the pit, put the pit into the spoon and carefully put the pit into my bowl without making a mess. I loved my first lesson. It tasted good.

A few days after I moved in, I found out that my uncle, Schneider Franz Vetter, had been hired out from the Labor Camp and worked kitty-corner across the street from the grocery store. I found out that Lisi lived with him and occasionally I was taken over there so we could play together. I was so happy to see her. I often wondered what had happened to her. After Oma had died, Lisi one day had disappeared; but no one could tell me anything about it.

Lisi told me how she was smuggled out. She said, "My father's (Franz Vetter) boss had a job assignment in Gakowa for the Partisans; and they both drove to Gakowa to do the job. When the job was completed, his boss picked up Lisi on the way back to Sombor and told the Partisan guard that was stationed at the exit of Gakowa that Lisi was his daughter. Since Lisi had long hair, because she managed to outrun the barber who clipped every one bald, the Partisan guard believed him and let them drive out

Irene also used to take me for walks in the city and I would walk next to her; but when she ran across someone that knew her, she would let me know by a signal and I would walk away from her and pretend I didn't know her and hung around in the distance until they were gone. Then I would resume my walk next to her.

One day as I was walking with Irene, she ran into someone she knew; and that person told her about a real horror story that happened the night before, at the Labor

Camp during the Partisans' drinking party. Everywhere we went, people were talking about it. The news spread all over town. Commandant Rajko was in trouble.

Heinous crimes toward the ethnic Germans, was supposed to be a hush, hush affair. It was not supposed to be spread world wide. Tito's Partisans had led us to the Death Camp taking farmers' roads not on main traveled roads where the public could see.

Commandant Rajko was proud and arrogant and very cruel. After people used to come back from their work assignment at night, they used to go behind the barracks in order to pray, hoping no one would see them praying. It was not allowed. When he saw people praying, he would say, "Yasam Bog!" (I'm your God). Go ahead and pray, it's useless; because things, here, go **MY** way!" He was also very cruel to his men in charge. There was never a smile seen on his face.

The Partisans slaughtered one ethnic German man the night before during one of their drinking parties in Commandant Rajko's Office building. It was a slow death for that poor man. The Partisans took the bayonet from their rifle and started to slice off the man's ears, then his nose, then his fingers, then his hand, then his arms; and then they stabbed him all over. Blood was, gushing everywhere. They hauled two women from the women's barracks to the scene who were forced to clean up the blood while they were slicing away on the man. The outcry of pain was so intense, that the screams were heard by everyone (the slave laborers) in the surrounding sleeping quarters in the Labor Camp. Mistreatments like this one brought fear to everyone interned at the Labor Camp; because no one knew whose turn was next. Tito's Partisans were real brutal – barbaric.

The blame for this incident was passed from Commandant Rajko to some of his Partisans in charge; and in return the accused Partisans squealed on Rajko for keeping some of the gold jewelry that was collected from the Germans in April of 1945 for himself, and not handing it all over to Tito's regime. This resulted in Commandant Rajko getting locked up in the Osna, a prison for convicted criminals. The Osna was located in Sombor. Since he was jailed for life, a new Commandant was put in his place at the Sombor Forced Labor Camp. The new Commandant ordered all hired out slave laborers to be returned to the Labor Camp as soon as possible.

Fear came over people in Sombor including the Bartlitsch family. They were now afraid of getting into trouble if anyone found out that they harbored an ethnic German child. My mother was informed that I had to leave.

Since my uncle, Schneider Franz Vetter, (Lisi and Franzi's father) was employed close by, Franz Vetter and Mami asked their employers for permission to take Lisi and me to our aunt, Nanni Neni Mihailowitsch. She lived close by, in Apatin on the Danube River. Because she had married a Serb, she was not put into a concentration camp and she got to keep her house. Her husband had died many years before.

Next morning, Mami and my uncle took us to Apatin by bike which they had borrowed from their employers. They dropped us off and immediately returned to their employers.

It was the only safe place for us to be. I had rarely seen my Dad's aunt, Nanni Neni, and it was hard for me to be with someone that I hardly knew. I was very shy. It was a good thing that Lisi and I were there together. We were put up in the bedroom toward the back of the house. Now we had to learn to speak Hungarian. We were not allowed to speak even one word in German. Being young, we learned quickly.

My habit, of closing mine eyes every time I put a spoon in my mouth, bothered my aunt greatly. It was a habit I created because I didn't want to look at the worms in my bowl of bean soup in Gakowa. When we ate and I closed my eyes, she used to say, "If you close your eyes again, I will hit you!" From the expression on her face, I knew she meant it. I was afraid of her. She had a stern look on her face. Therefore, every time I put the spoon to my mouth I'd open my eyes as wide as I could for fear of getting hit.

We arrived in Apatin beginning of April in 1946. I was very skinny and had red hair and a face full of freckles. Looking in the mirror, all I saw was my freckles. We did not have any mirrors in Gakowa; and therefore I never noticed my freckles. I must have said something to my aunt complaining about my freckles; because on Palm Sunday she told me that if I shook all the blooming apricot trees in her yard when the church bells rang, I would be rid of them. She had quite a few apricot trees. Palm Sunday arrived and upon hearing the church bells ring, I dashed out into the yard trying to shake all the little apricot trees in bloom while the church bells rang. I don't know however if it works. I don't know if I got to all the trees before the bells stopped ringing or not; because I still have my freckles. No comment!

On Easter Sunday Nanni-Neni, Lisi, and I went to worship and then we went to the cemetery to the grave where Nanni-Neni's husband was buried and we put flowers on the grave. I remember distinctly hearing a bird call Kuku-kuku-kuku. Nanni-Neni told us that a Kuku lays her eggs into the nest with the eggs of a different breed of bird to get hatched.

At Nanni Neni's, my job was to feed the chickens and take care of a little piglet that she bought. She also owned very peculiar looking chickens that she called "Schokatzle." They had black feathers all over; but all of the neck was completely bald without any feathers at all on the entire neck. But then, on top of the head, they had a thick bunch of black feathers pointing every which way; and it made them look like they had a bad hair day.

Every day after feeding the chickens I had to take the piglet out on the road to the mulberry trees and let it feed on the fallen berries till it was full. Then I put it into its stall. I enjoyed watching the little piglet vacuum up those mulberries and end up with a purple snout. I can't recall what Lisi's chores were. She is older than I. She probably helped in the kitchen.

In the summer Nanni Neni and I used to weed and hoe the garden. She used to show me the difference between weeds and herbs. She also had a huge black cherry tree in the yard. In July when the cherries ripened, she used to ask me if I would climb the tree to pick the cherries. I liked that better than weeding.

She could not pick them without a ladder because the tree was very tall; and she felt she was too old to climb up the ladder. I loved to climb that tree. I loved those big sweet cherries. The nicest ones were way at the very top; and I would climb all the way up. It made her very nervous when I climbed up that high; but I assured her that I would not fall down and she was very glad when I picked her the nicest ones from the top. Of course a lot of those cherries wound up in my stomach also.

Lisi and I had a lot of fun at Nanni Neni's eating those succulent red cherries and spitting the pits as far as we could. I remember when watermelons were turning ripe. I love watermelons. Lisi and I would eat them and have a contest to see who could spit the seeds the farthest. We had fun playing simple games. Spitting contests were our favorite entertainment.

While we lived there, we had no news of our Fathers and Mothers or siblings. Nanni Neni had a daughter named Nanshi. We called her Nanshi- Neni (aunt Anni). She was about the same age as my mother. She was not home very much because her husband was the captain of a ship that traveled up and down the Danube; and she mostly traveled with him. She came home only occasionally. I missed Dati and Mami and Joschi very much although Nanni Neni turned out to be real nice to us. However she was very strict.

My daily prayers to God kept ascending. I was confident that someday, someday I would be united again with my family. That someday came the end of August 1946 when Nanschi Neni took me on a train ride and told me she was taking me to Bereg to be with my family.

Before I left, I hugged Nanni Neni and Lisi and said, "Auf Wiedersehn." (Until we meet again).

I had gotten fond of Nanni Neni; but I was eager to leave to be with my family. When I left I had mastered the Hungarian language and I could speak it fluently. Dati was transferred from Gakowa to Bereg at the end of August 1946, because the town needed a barrel maker and Dati was allowed to have his family with him. God be thanked!

Chapter 11
Dati is Sent to Bereg

When we arrived in Bereg, we got off the train and Nanschi Neni took me to the house where Dati, Mami and Joschi were staying. They shared a small house with a friendly little old man. I was so happy to be together with my family. I thanked Nanschi Neni for bringing me there; and she left to go back to Apatin.

Although we were part of the labor camp in Bereg the housing with the old man was only temporary. When Dati and Mami were finished with their work for the day, I was curious as to how we all wound up in Bereg, even Mami, because she used to be in Sombor and was not allowed to be with Dati in Gakowa. While I lived in Apatin, I had not at all had any contact with my family. I was surprised that we all got to be together. Dati explained:

Last week an officer came to Gakowa from the town of Bereg, a Croatian town. He went to see Commandant Schutzo and inquired if there was a barrel maker in Gakowa. Bereg was surrounded by grape vineyards and the grape harvest was near. They were in need of new barrels to store the new wine in; and they had no barrel maker. Schutzo told him there was a barrel maker; because I had made him a table top version as a gift. He was ready to send me to

Bereg. I went to see Schutzo and told him that I would only go if I could take my wife and children along.

"That's out of the question!" Schutzo replied. "You know that I can shoot you if you refuse?" So I said, "Go ahead and shoot me! But, if you shoot me, they won't get a barrel maker!" So Schutzo thought about it and decided to let Mami, Joschi, and you come along.

I liked the old man who owned the little house. He was like a grandpa to me. He noticed that I had outgrown my shoes and always walked bare foot. He decided to make me a pair of wooden shoes. It was very interesting to watch him carve shoes out of a block of wood. Winter was not far away and I did not have to worry about walking barefoot in the snow. I thanked him with all my heart.

After some time, we were moved to another house and we shared a room with other people that were forced to work in Bereg. This town hired laborers from various forced labor camps to work their vineyards. The inhabitants were Schokatzen (Croatian), real nice friendly people.

The food for the workers was quite a bit better than in Gakowa. We now had pea soup every day three times a day, with quite a lot of peas in it and only an occasional bug which could easily be fished out. After all, hard working people needed food to be able to work the vineyards and work the wood for the barrels.

My Dad's first job was to make barrels for one very kind-hearted Croatian family. They used to provide lunch for Dati and then give him some extra food to take home to his family. That was a welcome treat for us kids from the daily serving of pea soup. Occasionally, they sent some mutton meat home with my dad so we could have a treat.

But it was not a treat for us. We never ever ate mutton before. My mother attempted to cook it to the best of her abilities (my Mom is a very good cook); but it had such a strong sheepish odor; it permeated the whole room. We had a hard time eating it. Give me pea soup anytime. That was the thought of my whole family.

My uncle, Schneider Franz Vetter, was sent to Bereg to help my father with the barrels because the demand for wine barrels was so great. He was also allowed to bring along my aunt, Rosl-Bas (my dad's youngest sister), Lisi, and Franzi who had nicely recovered from typhoid. He was sick for a long, long time. They came some time later on. They also agreed that mutton was no favorite of theirs, either. Not that we were not grateful for their gift. It's what in the heart that counts. Mutton has a peculiar smell that we just could not get used to.

Mami's job in Bereg was to milk the cows, clean out the stalls, and gather the wheat for a farmer. That was her job all the while we were in Bereg. When Dati finished all the barrels for a certain family before it was night time, they let him go back to camp; and then he could do whatever he wanted to until the next day when someone else hired him. He did not get paid. They paid the state of Yugoslavia for his work. Whenever Dati got off early, he and I went fishing or swimming. The Partisans were not as strict with the workers. While we were in Bereg, Dati made friends with the judge of the town. He was a real nice man. Everyday he used to bring us a liter of milk for us to drink. During the very busy grape harvest, Dati used to work in the yard of the town hall. Anyone, that had problems with a barrel that had a leak, could bring it to the town hall square and Dati would fix it. The town's folk liked him very much.

During several conversations with the judge, Dati expressed his hope for this bad time of war to end and his desire to soon be able to return to his home in Sentiwan with his family. To this the judge replied, "Henrich, you have no future anymore here in Yugoslavia since you're German. Tito is trying to cleanse Yugoslavia of all ethnic Germans. Go to the land of your ancestors."

Sundays were a day off except for Mami; she still had to milk the cows, clean out the stalls and tend to her work for most of the day. We could pretty much go wherever we wanted to around town as long as we were all back in our room for a nightly head count at 11:00 PM to make sure no one escaped. Bereg was located near the Danube River; and an arm of the Danube River was the border mark between Yugoslavia and Hungary. Partisan guards were stationed all along the border with little huts at certain distances to have some shelter in inclement weather. They used to walk back and forth from one hut to the other guard's hut, - about a half mile apart -exchange a short conversation and head back to their own hut. This walking back and forth went on all day long and all night long, getting a replacement at the end of their shift. Their job was to make sure no one would cross over the border and escape into Hungary. If you escaped into Hungary, you were free

Every Sunday we went fishing and swimming and my dad would greet the guards in their native language and ask them how they were. He could speak the Serbian language real well and got quite friendly with them. My Dad used to love to joke around with people; and they began to look forward to seeing him; and he used to have quite lengthy conversations with them. It broke up their boring job of just walking back and forth in practically the same spot every day.

The purpose of going fishing and swimming was for my dad to feel out the river. He noticed it was deep in some places and quite shallow in another part. In the shallow place one could just wade across. That gave him an idea. He noted the shallow part by looking at the landmarks. He had an escape plan but kept it to himself. By having a lot of conversations with the Partisan guards, he knew exactly their comings and goings.

On one occasion, during their conversation, he asked them "What do you do if it rains real hard? I guess you don't have a pleasant job walking in the rain and getting soaked to your bone?" "Well" they answered: "If it rains real hard, we just stay in our huts." Dad had his escape plan complete. "We'll escape when it rains real hard" was his thought - but this had to wait till next spring. He kept this plan to himself. He didn't even tell my mother what he was planning. It was already fall and the grape harvest was in full swing. It took hours and hours to get all the barrels ready. Besides, it was not a good idea to escape in winter. All our clothes were worn out from constant wear. The wooden sandals my Dad had made from a flat piece of wood with leather straps cut from an old worn-out pair of leather shoes, was not fit footwear for walking in snow in winter. His plan had to wait.

Winter arrived with lots of snow. Schneiders also lived with us in the same living quarters. Dad had a suggestion that we toughen up so we won't get so sick in winter. He said, "Let's go outside with our coats on, and, run barefoot in the snow once around the yard. The first one in is the winner.

That sounded awful; but my dad convinced us that it would be fun. He'd be the leader. We had a lot of fun with Dati even in bad times; so why not; let's give it a try. We all put our coats on, Dati, Joschi, Lisi, Franzi and I and dashed into the snow barefooted.

Rosl-Bas and Mami stayed in the warm with towels, waiting to dry our feet when we came in.

What a shock! The snow was icy, it felt like stepping on needles; but Dati said, "Whoever got in the house first was the winner!" We ran so fast we could hardly feel the snow; and he made sure we made it into the room ahead of him.

When we came into the warm, we didn't care who the winner was. Our feet itched so badly and tingled from thawing out, we were just so glad we were in the warm room. He made life fun in spite of all the misery. When Lisi and I get together, nowadays, and I mention about the time we ran barefoot through the snow, we just look at each other and smile.

Bereg was a better place to be in winter; because the room we stayed was heated, unlike Gakowa; there was no heat in the winter and we kept warm by huddling together and constantly rubbing our limbs go get circulation going. The room in Bereg had a tile oven built into the outside wall of the room. One had to go outside and put wood in and that would heat up the tile inside the room and gentle warmth would radiate throughout the room.

Winter was spent by telling stories of life from all the different places that the folk sharing our room came from.

We also tried to make up a song with a funny verse about each person in the room, one that would be funny and make us laugh. Out of thirty verses, I still remember one: "Unser Priza hot Kloset Papier mit Reslein, unser Priza is a ganz moderner Herr". Translated, "Our barber uses toilet paper with roses, with roses, with roses – our barber is a very successful man."

Winter ended and spring arrived and so did the month of April with its showers. It would have been a good time to escape if we had money to buy food. We had to wait until the farmers were in need of workers to hoe the corn fields so my parents would be able to find work and would get paid. We had to wait until May was Dati's thought.

One day it just poured and poured; it rained cats and dogs without end. It was in May 1947. Dadi called his family together when no one was around and whispered that: "If this rain keeps up, we would try to escape after the 11:00 p.m. headcount." All of a sudden I could feel fear rising from my toes and radiating upward and throughout every inch of my body; and I could feel a big lump stuck in my throat. All I could think of at that moment was my friend, Leni, who was killed with a pitch fork.

Dati said, "No one must know about our plan. After everyone in the room is asleep; we'll get up one by one as if we had to go to the outhouse; and then the four of us would sneak out of the house and sneak down the streets and through the field to the spot he picked out. There was a shallow spot where we could just wade across to freedom."

Evening came. The guard came at 11:00 p.m. to take a head count. Every one was accounted for and he left. After we thought everyone in the room was asleep, Mom and I got up and went outside. When my brother; and Dati started, a man suddenly sat up and said, "I know what you're up to. If you don't take us all with you, we're going to call the soldiers on you!" Dati had no choice. He told them to sneak out and meet us in front of the house. We all would have to walk hand in hand because it was dark so we wouldn't get separated from one another.

My heart was pounding from fear of being found out. It was raining steadily and we all were holding hands and trying to keep up with the person ahead of us. Dati was the only one knowing where to go and admonished everyone not to talk. I was scared of getting caught. I can't remember how far we walked. I only know that fear took over my emotions.

Most of the people could not swim; so my dad told them to make sure to stay behind him when we arrived at the river; so that all crossed the shallow place where one could simply wade across. There were no street lights in those days in that small town. Everybody gave their word and we proceeded.

When we approached the river, my dad mentioned that we were getting close. When they heard the words "getting close," the people that accompanied us, let go of their grip, raced past us and plunged into the river - not heeding my father's advice to stay behind him.

Suddenly there was a loud scream, as the people plunged into the ice cold water up to their necks - because they now were in the deep part of the river. My heart pounded - it seemed to leap out of my throat. There was so much noise the people were making, fighting the water with their hands. I surely thought the guards were coming any moment to riddle us down with their bullets.

Was this our last moment alive? Total fear overcame me. "Oh God, Our Father in heaven! Please! I don't want to die. Please help us!" (My thoughts in prayer). The noise of the people all around us was loud enough to instantly summon the Partisan guards.

Dati with me on his arm stood at the rivers edge and motioned for Mami and Joschi to cross over to make sure they had no trouble crossing. We made long hurried strides to swiftly wade across and hopefully reach the other side before getting detected by the guards. We had to climb up the bank and we tried to hurry with all our might.

As we were climbing up the bank, the weight of the backpack on Dati's back threw him off balance and we both fell backwards into the water and had to struggle to make it up the bank again.

Water was pouring from the sky and the icy river sent chills throughout my body. We were totally soaked through and through when we finally reached the other side - freedom. The noise of the people splashing got less and less. Then all of a sudden there was total silence, an eerie feeling of total silence.

Then little by little we could hear hushed whispers of joy and whispers of praises to God. (Gott sei Dank! Gott sei Dank!) As everyone gathered to the sound of whispers. With a quick head count, we knew that we all made it. We all safely reached the other side to freedom. Dati told every one, "You're on your own!" With quick goodbyes, there was no time to waste, to get as far away from the border as possible and out of the range of gun fire......just in case....

Then the sound of "thud-cluck , thud-cluck, thud cluck was heard as everyone tried to run across the muddy field as fast as they could, to get away from the river's edge and dispersed into the unknown darkness, everyone going their own way whichever way they thought best.

It was hard to run across the rain-soaked muddy fields. When one sank one's foot into the soil it squished and it was hard to pull the foot out of the mud, the mud did not want to let go. It still poured from the sky. It was so cold my whole body shook and my teeth began to chatter; but it was OK. We were alive. Thank God! We were alive. We kept on going, hoping to find some kind of shelter from the rain. We dragged along. It was very tiring, but we kept on. It slowly began to dawn and in the distance we detected a building. As we got closer we stumbled upon a small barn.

It was empty except for a big pile of straw. We went in and sank our weary bodies into the dry straw and pulled it over us up to our neck; to try to get warm and rest from our exhausting walk.

When the sun began to rise, we heard footsteps. My heart began to race. Who could it be? Instantly we all jumped to our feet ready for the unpleasant.

The straw fell off. The door opened and two eyes stared at us in surprise. The farmer, the owner of the hut looked us over one by one. His eyes fixed on me - scrawny, skin and bones, hollow eyes, wet hair plastered to my head - and his expression changed from shock to tenderness.

He rushed to make a fire so we could dry our clothes and warm up, and then he left to get us some food. We knew we had nothing to fear when he left; because the way he talked to Dati and his compassionate behavior showed in his eyes. We knew he could be trusted. He returned with blankets, warm milk and bread and towels.

Part II
Mami's Story

I was born Knoebl, Elisabeth on November 12, 1912, in Batschsentiwan, Hungary in the Province of Batschka. My father's name was Andreas and my mother's was Rosalia (maiden name, Mack). I have a brother six years younger than I, named Andres.

It was the custom in our region to marry at a young age. I fell in love with a handsome young man named Heinrich but called "Henrich". His family name was Stefan. There were so many families named "Stefan" in our town that each one had to have a nickname to identify who was who. Therefore people chose the trade of the man as their nickname. Henrich was a barrel maker by trade. Therefore his nickname was "Binder" Henrich.

After a brief courtship, we decided to get married. However, a young man could not get married unless he first served as a soldier in the Serbian army for at least nine months. When his duty was completed, we planned our wedding day for April 16, 1929. We had a large wedding as the custom was in our town. It took three days of baking and cooking for this festive occasion. Many friends and relatives helped. Henrich was 21 and I was 16.

When the big day arrived, according to our custom, Henrich picked me up from my house bringing along the town's band followed by a crowd of relatives, friends, and neighbors. We walked hand in hand to the church to get married, and were followed by the band and a huge crowd, trailing. After the ceremony we had a big dinner, while the band was playing. All, who followed to the ceremony, were invited to the feast. It took a lot of food.

It was also the custom for the new bride to move into the house of the groom's family. We lived with my Stefan in-laws for ten years. Henrich and his father had a prosperous business, making and repairing wine barrels and wooden tubs of various sizes.

Our marriage was blessed with two lovely children, a boy named Josef and called Joschi and a girl named Elisabeth and called Lisl. We lived a peaceful life until World War II broke out; and little by little trouble started.

This is a sequence of major events from 1918-1944. At the end of World War I, the Treaty of Trianon was signed June 4, 1920. The terms of the Treaty took territory from Hungary and awarded it to Serbia, thus creating a new country called Yugoslavia. There were five Provinces that Hungary had to give up: Baranja, Batschka, Banat, Syrmia, and Slavonia. Since our town was located in the Province of Batschka, we now automatically belonged to Yugoslavia. The name of our town, Batschsentiwan, was changed to the Serbian name Prigrevitza Sveti Ivan.

There were many problems with the change-over in the beginning because of the borderline created by the Treaty. It divided some towns because the border ran through the middle of the town. Half of the town was located in

Hungary and the other half in Yugoslavia. This was also the case with people's farms. Half of their land was in one country and the other half in another. One could not claim dual citizenship. If the house where one lived stood on land awarded to Yugoslavia, then one became an automatic citizen of Yugoslavia. Even though the rest of one's property was in Hungary, you could not consider yourself a citizen of Hungary.

When Yugoslavia took over, those ethnic German, who, prior, were Hungarian citizens were given automatic citizenship of Yugoslavia. This border change created a few problems in the beginning; but we learned to live with the changes – life went on. We lived in Yugoslavia peaceful for more than 20 years and got along well with our Slavic and Magyar neighbors.

Germany and Yugoslavia were friendly after WW I. Every evening at 7:00 PM, the Belgrade Radio station broadcast German songs over the air featuring Marlene Dietrich singing the song, "Lili Marlen" and others. We enjoyed listening to the nightly broadcast, followed by the news.

Then in 1939 WW II broke out. Adolf Hitler began to attack and invade the countries that closely surrounded Germany. One by one Germany began to occupy Poland, Czechoslovakia, Russia, and Hungary. Even though war was all around us, life in our town continued its usual peaceful way.

On Easter Sunday in April 1941, Hitler bombed Belgrade and took over the town. Bombings in our area were unheard of. My husband and his close friends were curious and rode the train to Belgrade to see the devastation. There were German troops every where and parts of Belgrade had been reduced to rubble. They could not believe what they saw. That incident put Germany and Hungary at war with Yugoslavia.

The "Honved" (the Hungarian army) advanced into the Province of Batschka and occupied it all along the Danube River down to Novi Sad, gained victory over it, and reclaimed it back for Hungary. Now again, we belonged to Hungary; and the name of the town was changed back to Batschsentiwan (Sentiwan for short). The Province of Batschka was the only province that the Hungarian army occupied. Across the Danube in the Province of Baranja, the German army already held a stronghold; and the Province of Banat was occupied by German soldiers as well.

From that time on, things did not look good for the future of the ethnic German Danube Swabians. Danube Swabians is the name by which the descendents of the ethnic German settlers were known who immigrated to the Panonian lowlands of Hungary 200 years ago.

Some young folks in town started to form a German cultural group and called it "Deutscher Kulturbund." They wore German uniforms. Even a large group of women participated and began to march throughout the town trying to recruit people into their group and persuade the men of Sentiwan to volunteer and join the German army. Whoever refused was nicknamed, "Die Schwarzen" (The Black Ones).

Most of the older men of our town thought it foolish to volunteer to go to war if one didn't have to join; especially, for another country.

Our neighbor, Burghardt Leopold Vetter, a WW I veteran, said to my husband, "Henrich don't volunteer. You will never see your family again if you are sent to Russia to fight. It's a vast country with bitter cold winters. Most of my war buddies in WW I froze to death, fighting there." He came home after spending ten years in Siberia as a POW.

Even my father advised Henrich not to join. Most people in town were not impressed with Hitler's propaganda. It was the young men of our town that pressed the issue. They were indoctrinated by the Nazi propaganda that occupied Banat. They tried to convince our young men to fight for their Vaterland (the land of our ancestors – Germany) – to help them win the war.

Even my brother, Andres, joined the German army despite the advice of our father against it. He left without saying good bye. My father found out about him joining a few days later. This put a heavy burden on his heart.

My father had been diagnosed with an inoperable aneurysm on his main artery to the heart a few years prior. He was employed as a sworn-in advocate for the town's Serbian court and was the mediator when legal problems arose between ethnic Germans and Serbs. He was respected by all citizens for doing a good job.

In 1938 he had to resign because the aneurysm was already pressing on his voice box and the doctor advised him against handling any strenuous situations. The news that Andres was sent to Russia to fight was too much grief for my father to bear and he became bedridden. He died with a burst artery in February 1943 not seeing his son again.

The members of the Kulturbund approached my husband many times and tried to press him to join. He continually refused to volunteer. He did not want to leave his family and his very prosperous business on a voluntary enlistment basis. He said, "My ancestors, who came and settled here to start a new life, poured sweat and blood into this new land to make it productive and provide a good home for their family therefore; I'm staying.

The majority of the inhabitants of Sentiwan (7,000) were ethnic Germans. Only the town officials and the schools were controlled by the government. The language of instruction in school was German; however, one had to learn to speak the Hungarian language or Serbo-Croation depending on which country ruled.

As the war between Germany and Russia got more intense, the men of Sentiwan were pressured even more by the cultural group to join the German army. All the men that belonged to the "Kultur-Bund" had joined. Because my husband still refused, he was labeled as "a Black One."

Things began to get nasty. Many times young men, members of the Kultur Bund, lay in wait and beat up those who refused, including family members. That was done after dark when no one suspected. They also painted a big swastika on the front of the house of those who did not volunteer - at night, when people were sleeping. It happened to our house many times.

Seeing the swastika painted on our house upon wakening, made me want to scream. When Henrich saw it in the mornings, he would call, "Lisi get the white wash and get rid of it." I became angry every time I saw it because it made extra work for me since I had to paint over it repeatedly to make it disappear. This happened again and again.

In June each year, the people of Sentiwan celebrated Kirchweih Sunday. Each town had such a celebration, held on the anniversary of the dedication of their church. Solemn High Mass and devotions marked the religious activities, and a carnival followed.

This was such a Sunday in June, 1944. Every one looked forward to celebrating. The brass band played all afternoon and into evening. Children looked forward to riding on the carousel. There were all kinds of booths with various things to buy. The "Pretzel Man" walked through the crowded streets carrying a long pole with dozens of soft pretzels strung around the pole, for hungry people to buy.

People were visiting from neighboring towns. There was the sound of hustle and bustle of people talking and music playing and children screaming, enjoying the carousel ride. To sum it up – it was a fun day.

My husband's cousin and his wife came from Djakovo to visit us on this festive day and were planning to take the train back that evening. We had enjoyed the day and their visit. Time flew by and it was beginning to get dusk and time for them to leave.

Henrich decided to walk with them to the railroad station and see them off, since we rarely got to see them. He was planning to come home when the train pulled away.

I had put the children to bed and expected him home any minute. I waited and waited; but he did not come home the time I thought he would. The hand on the clock already pointed to 12:00 midnight and still there was no sight of Henrich. I began to wonder what kept him so long.

Tomorrow was a work day; and that meant rising early. He was not one for goofing off.

Another hour went by —and still there was no Henrich. Was he in trouble? It was not like him to come home late when he needed to rise early for work. I checked in on the children. They were sound asleep. Finally, I decided to walk over to my in-laws to see if perhaps he was there. I had to find out what kept him.

When I arrived at their house, I stood at the door listening for sounds inside. I hesitated to knock in case they were already sleeping. There was not a sound to be heard. They were sleeping. I really did not want to waken them; but I was beside myself with worry. Softly I knocked, hoping my mother-in-law would hear. Soon the door opened and she looked at me with surprise, since I came by myself at this time of night. I explained to her what had transpired. Now she also was worried. We needed to find him.

Since it had been a festive day, there were people still in the streets visiting with one another. We decided to look for him. We checked out the Inns in our neighborhood. No one had seen him. None of the people in the streets we met had seen him. Everyone in our town knew everyone living there.

We were getting worried. All the places we checked out were dead ends. "We may as well go home and wait," Henrich's mother said. "You should be home with the children".

I finally walked her home, reassuring her that I would let her know as soon as he came home. Then I went home to the children who were sleeping and had no idea that their father was missing.

I was a nervous wreck all night long. Where could he be? Did he get beaten up? It had happened to others who were marked as "The Black Ones." I prayed all night long for his protection. I finally fell asleep and woke up when his business partner, Tettman Stefan, showed up for work and started hammering away on a new barrel. I walked across the yard and stepped into the workshop and greeted him with, "Gudi Mar-ya!" (Good morning!)

Stefan immediately asked, "Where is Henrich, is he sick?"

I fought back tears when I told him what transpired last night. We were contemplating what to do next when I saw the children walking across the brick driveway heading toward the summer kitchen, which was next to the workshop. I stepped out the door and headed for the kitchen. They were hungry.

I decided to make them cream of wheat for breakfast and listened to their chatter, about what a fun day they had yesterday. I tried not to show that I was worried. Their father was usually already working when they arose. They had no clue as to what all happened while they were sleeping. I did not let on that anything was wrong. After they had finished eating, I headed back toward the work shop.

Stefan came out into the yard when he saw me coming. It was now already about 9:00 a.m. We were standing outside by the door, talking and looking toward our front gate to the yard when, guess who, comes walking through the gate?

"Well, here he comes," Stefan said. And there was Henrich walking into the yard still dressed in his Sunday best suit and wearing his Sunday shoes and smiling. I never saw a more wonderful sight. I ran over to him and hugged him and raised the big questions, "Where have you been? What happened last night? Why did you not come home?"

With his arms around me, we walked back to where Stefan was standing; and we all went into the workshop to talk privately. He proceeded to tell us what happened on his way back from the railroad station.

"I was on my way home from the railroad station; and as I came near Schoenberger's Inn, I noticed Schoenberger Toni standing out back waving his arms frantically. When he caught my attention, he put one finger over his lips and beckoned with his other hand to come. So I hurried over to him. He motioned for me not to speak and pulled me with his arm inside one of their bedrooms and closed the door. He whispered that he wanted to hide me because I was in danger of being beaten up."

"Oh, Henrich," I uttered. Then he continued.

Henrich explained, "While Toni was serving some of his guests at the inn, he overheard three young men talking of how they had been stalking me." Toni said, "They were planning to sneak up on you on your way back from the railroad station. When you passed the inn, they would beat the daylights out of you for not enlisting. They had been here quite a while. They wanted to surprise you in the dark when no one could see what they were up to. I want you to stay overnight in my bedroom. No one will know that you are here; and tomorrow morning during broad daylight, you can walk home as if nothing had happened. This way you will be safe; and Lisi, I'm sure will understand and be grateful. Toni is a good friend."

Henrich went into the house changed clothes and came into the workshop ready for work. As they were talking, Tettman Stefan said to Henrich, "You know, they are after me also. We need to get our heads together and come up with a plan on what to do. Soon, it will be mandatory to enlist, either to the German or Hungarian army. Time is running out. The September deadline will be here before we know it."

Henrich replied, "You know, with this enlisting business, one thing is for sure; now you know who your friends are. If you thought you had a good friend and he sees you coming down the street; and he knows you're coming toward him; all of a sudden he crosses the street and walks past you on the other side and doesn't acknowledge your presence – you know for sure."

Stefan agreed. "Isn't it sad that it had to come to this?" Henrich continued, "It is blind hate and misunderstanding - to hate someone, just because someone else does - not thinking whether it is right or wrong – just following the crowd." This said - they both started to work.

A few days later an opportunity such as Stefan and Henrich were looking for came up. Gloegl Toni from Apatin, a neighboring town, (not Schoenberger Toni from the Inn) came to visit us. It was unusual because we never saw him or his family in the summer time, only in winter. We were good friends because Toni's father and Henrich's father were war buddies in WW I.

We used to hitch up the horses to our sleigh and take a ride to Apatin to participate in their spinning and knitting get-togethers. They had a great big room with spinning wheels and a weaver's loom. Every week during winter they invited a group of friends to their home. The women would either knit or spin wool or weave while the children helped - holding the yarn or getting new spindles for those spinning the wool. The men sat around telling jokes or war stories. The time most often ended with everyone singing our favorite songs. It was a fun way to pass the dreary days of winter.

Toni proceeded to tell us that he was employed by the Hungarian army's repair crew who worked at the Stuhlweissenburg (Szekesfehervar) airport, in Hungary. He had just come home on his furlough. Toni thought that Henrich might be interested to join their repair crew.

Stuhlweissenburg (Szekesfehervar) had a big airport and when the Russians dropped bombs, the repair crew came in and fixed the damage and also dug fox holes for the protection of the Hungarian soldiers. The repair crew strictly worked locally. No one was ever sent to Russia; and it was close to home – only 50 Km (32 miles) away. Henrich and Stefan both told Toni they were interested and asked him to inquire if the repair crew had a spot for five new men.

After a good visit, Toni left. Henrich and Stefan resumed their work making barrels and spent the rest of the day in a good mood. About a month later, Henrich received a letter from Toni stating that they all can come anytime they were ready. They could use five new men.

Henrich in the meantime had talked to his three close friends about joining the repair crew. They all were interested. However, they had to leave without anyone knowing where they were going. Henrich made arrangements with Gerber Franz, our crop sharer, to come to our house with his wagon and pick up a sack stuffed with his clothes, and do the same for his three friends and Stefan. Then on August 2 at midnight, Gerber Franz was to come with the wagon and bring the sacks of clothes and meet them on the road, which lead to the city of Sombor, the Province Capital.

They all would be waiting by the statue located just outside of Sentiwan. The agreement was that Franz would pick them up and drive them to the railroad station in Sombor so they could take the train to Stuhlweissenburg (Szekesfehervar). No one in town would know that they left.

At the appropriate time for Henrich to leave, we parted with a hug and a kiss and he blew a kiss toward the children while they were sleeping. I was the only one that knew that he was leaving; otherwise our lives could have been in danger. Henrich told me that he would send me a telegram when they reached their destination. His proof to me, that they had arrived safely, would be a message that stated "Rosa geht mit." translated "Rosa is joining us." No one else would get a telegram. I would let the other wives know that they were safe.

It was so hard for me to see him leave. I remembered the frenzy that I was in when he didn't come home that night in June when I didn't know what had happened to him. Now it is all over again – the not knowing. I prayed with all my heart for his safety. I went to bed; but I had difficulty falling asleep.

The next few days I was barraged with questions from friends and neighbors as to the "whereabouts of Henrich." My answer was, "I don't know." The children missed their father and wanted an explanation. It was hard not being able to tell the children where their father was. We prayed for his safety - wherever he was.

News, that Henrich was missing, traveled fast throughout Sentiwan. By this time, the German SS were in charge at the town hall. When the news spread that Henrich was gone, two German SS soldiers paid me a visit demanding that I tell where my husband was. I insisted that I did not know. (The lives of my children were in danger). I insisted that I did **not** know.

Several days after the SS visited me, I received a paper from the town hall. It was a summons for me to report to them the next day. I began to get worried. That afternoon a young boy came to our house with a note from a man working in the town hall. The man had worked with my father in the court before he had to take a medical leave. The note read, "Lisi don't go, they are going to beat you up. Ignore the summons." I took his advice and did not report. That was the last time I was threatened.

A few days later, I received a telegram. The message read, "Rosa geht mit." I was so relieved. He was safe. "Gott sei Dank!" - Thanks be to God!

The front was getting closer and closer, now the September deadline of mandatory enlistment had arrived. All men up to age sixty had to join the German army. When the train took them away, the town was left with only the very elderly men, women and their children to carry on the work of the household, farmland, vineyards and cattle. It was tough on the women. Grape harvest was coming near. That was a lot of work. When finished, the grape vines had to be heeled over with dirt before winter arrived to keep the root stock from freezing during winter. That was a back-breaking job.

October arrived, that would have been the highlight of the grape harvest in previous years. With the men all gone, it was an enormous task for women, now impossible. Because it had been raining daily for three weeks, the fields were muddy. All we picked of the grapes was for eating.

Chapter 12
The Red Army on the Way to the Front

During the night toward the latter part of October 1944, while we were sleeping, Russian soldiers had come into our town. Horse-drawn wagons were trying to head toward the Danube River to the Russian front. It had been raining hard during the night. It was a surprise to wake up in the morning to sounds of yelling and cursing in Russian. The language is similar to the Serbo-Croation we were used to hearing; but I could tell the difference. I could not believe what I saw when I looked out the window. There were Russian soldiers, both men and women soldiers, sitting on the wagons whipping the horses to try to make them pull harder. Due to the rain, the wagon wheels of the Red Army became buried half way up the wheels in muck. Our street up to the middle of town was a dirt road. Then the stone street started. With ammunition on their wagons, they were lined up one wagon behind the other from the road they had entered Sentiwan, all the way past our house and up to the church. Our street was a muddy mess. The wheels of their wagons were imbedded and would not budge. The horses could not pull the wagons out of the mud. Not being able to move on, they began to break into houses in search for guns and plundering our homes, and taking anything they wanted.

They came into our home, lay on our beds with their muddy boots and soiled our beautiful white down comforters, not caring about the mess they made. It made me sick how within a few minutes they turned our house into shambles. The women soldiers went through our closets and took my beautiful dresses and jackets that were for worship on Sundays. From fright, I was frozen to the spot in our bedroom and could not move. The children had expressions of fear written all over their faces so we just stood there mute. We did not want to do anything stupid. We just watched in disbelief. They took whatever caught their eye and left in search for other houses to plunder. In whatever house they found a gun, the owner of the house was either beaten severely or shot to death.

My husband owned a gun because he used to go rabbit hunting. He hid it in a concealed spot in the pig pen; but showed me where he put it before he left for Stuhlweissenburg (Szekesfehervar). Fear took hold of me when I heard what they did to people where they found one; and I wrecked my brain, all day, for a way to dispose of it before being found in our home, just in case other Russians came and thoroughly searched our house.

I could not fall asleep that night, tossing and turning. How could I possibly get rid of it with all those wagons in our street? I waited till late into the night, could wait no longer. I had to get rid of it while the soldiers were sleeping. I finally got up, trying not to waken the children.

Carefully I opened the bedroom door, stepped outside and headed for the pig pen. I retrieved the gun from its hiding place and tip-toed toward our front gate. My heart was pounding – should I or should I not? What if I got caught? What will happen to the children? I waited and listened for the right moment that I thought the soldiers were all sleeping. I don't remember how long I stood there trembling.

I finally mustard up enough courage and told myself "this is it!" Carefully opening the gate, I peaked out into the street. There was dead silence. It was dark and I heard no one. One thing in my favor was the brick sidewalk in front of the houses on our street. I could walk barefoot not worrying about the "cluck" sound made if one walked through the mud.

I took a step outside. There was total silence. Russians in the wagon in front of our house seemed to be sleeping. My heart was pounding. I turned my head to the right and looked toward the faint rays of the street light in the distance which revealed no one down the street. So I took a step to the right and slowly sneaked with gun in hand past their wagons about three houses down and laid the gun into a muddy rut, hastily pulled mud over it. Nobody would know whose gun it was. It was such a muddy mess. I was able to get rid of it without making a sound. Then I sneaked, oh so carefully, back into our yard and into our bedroom where the children were sleeping. Did I ever thank God that night! I don't remember how long the soldiers were stuck until they were able to move; but everyone was greatly relieved when they finally moved on.

The women and men over sixty years old carried on the necessary work in the fields and vineyards. Field corn had to be harvested and the root stock of the grapevines had to be covered with dirt to keep them from freezing during winter. Pumpkins had to be stored. There was a lot of hard work for women to do without their men.

In the distance, one could hear the sound of thunder from the roaring of the cannons. Women in our town were glad that our village was not involved with the daily activities of war just 7 km away.

On November 1, 1944 troops of Russian soldiers accompanied by Tito's Partisans marched into our town and occupied it. They celebrated victory with drinking and shooting. Thousands of Russian soldiers marched toward the front on the shores of the Danube River to set up their gunnery and cannons. Many Russian soldiers were housed in our homes in Sentiwan. That's when chaos began. I was fortunate that I did not have to house any soldiers. The women soon found out what we had been spared for so long – what war entailed.

The Russians soon let us know that they were in charge. The inhabitants of Sentiwan were commanded daily to bring various items to the town square for the use of the Russian army – radios, bicycles, meat, and all kinds of food. Items asked for, via the drummer, had to be brought or severe punishment was dealt out. Then again an order went out via the town crier that all young men and women fit for work had to report daily to the town square for "Rabota!" That means to work in Russian. Those fit for work were sent to the Danube River which flowed through our region 7 Km from Sentiwan.

The Russian front was on the shores of the Danube River near Apatin. The river flooded the area after the last heavy rain and made it difficult for the Red Army to set up their cannons. I was in the group fit for work. When we arrived there, we had to cut and gather corn stalks from the surrounding corn fields, and also collect tree stumps and branches and carry them to put in place to dam up the shore.

The Danube River flooded during heavy rainfall because that region was low land and had to be dammed up so that the Russian gunnery could drive on it and not sink in. The Red Army had been delayed in their advancement because of the mud in the area.

It took three whole days of laying down cornstalks and tree stumps so that the gunnery and wagons could move on and Stalin's cannon be set in place. When our work was done, they sent us home and immediately firing began.

The German army lay across the Danube River in the Province of Baranja which they had occupied. Russia's best defense system, the Stalin's cannon was placed on our side of the Danube, shooting across the Danube River at the German army on the other side. Stalin's multi-barrel cannon, was called Stalin's Organ because the sound of it when fired resonated like an organ. It shot continuously day and night, causing a lot of casualties. It was so powerful that we could feel the earth tremble in our town. There were a lot of casualties on both sides. Thousands of Russian soldiers had to be buried.

From then on a group of able bodied men and women had to report daily to the airstrip for work of one type or another. Some had to clear the runway, others cleaned up the surrounding fields, the rest were sent to the head slave Labor Camp in Sombor which sent them to the hospital to take care of the wounded.

Russian soldiers and Tito's Partisans were the only ones accepted at the hospital for treatment. The hospital completely refused all medical treatment for German folk, whether men, women, or child. No one physically able to work could refuse the daily work duties from the Russian army without suffering severe bodily harm.

From then on, fear came over the women living in Sentiwan and night time was dreaded since the Russian soldiers returned from the airport always drunk, looking for someone to rape. This was a nightly occurrence. Therefore the women decided to band together and make a pact that when hearing a woman scream when being attacked, every woman in town would go out into the street and scream with all her might and keep on screaming as loud as she could. This screaming created a weird sound and confused the drunken soldiers and thus lessened the rapes somewhat.

We were afraid to sleep in our bedroom; so Joschi, Lisl, and I slept in one bed in our summer kitchen instead - to make them believe no one was home. We dared not to turn on any light. Evenings we just sat in the dark. Often we slept at our neighbor's house. It was a time of hiding. Whenever we heard the Russians coming, we ran out of the house and hid in different places – in the pig pen, the hay loft. Night time was dreaded. They raped women young and old. They did not care about their age. At the edge of our town, there are just a few houses. One night seven Russian soldiers went into one house and all seven of them raped the woman in that house. In another house they violated a mother and her daughter at the same time. Many unmentionable things were done to women. It was a time of constant fear and constant hiding.

Toward the end of November 1944, the drummer marched through Sentiwan announcing that he had a message from the government. Everyone needed to come and hear the new law that went into effect November 21, 1944 at Jajce, Bosnia.

As people gathered around him he yelled out, "The law declares that all persons of German ancestry living in Yugoslavia, regardless of previous political loyalties or anti-Nazi actions are stripped of their citizenship; and all farms, vineyards, estates, cattle and any other goods will be confiscated and given to the Serbs. It declares that ethnic Germans have lost all their rights and legal protection. The only exception was if a person of German ancestry had married someone that was not a German – for instance, a Hungarian, Gypsy or Serb."

After the town crier finished reading the new law, he did a double beat on his drum to signal the end of his message and then walked on, beating the regular beat of the drum until he reached the next stop at the corner of the main street and cross street, calling townsfolk to assemble to hear his message.

Everyone lingered in the street discussing the outcome of this new law. We were all perplexed. It was unbelievable what all of us on our street just heard. All kinds of comments and questions were repeated over and over in disbelief. "Did we hear right?"

"The announcement meant that we lost our Yugoslavian citizenship, our house, our farms, our vineyards, our cattle and anything we owned. Everything would be given to the Serbs. Everything we worked so hard for all our life. We could not be treated by a doctor, or get medicine, or take a train or ride a bus. Simply put, we had no rights. If someone wanted to move into our house, we had to give it to them. Whatever we had could be taken away in the blink of an eye.

"What is going on?" people asked. "Who is responsible for this?"

I heard our neighbor say, "Tito!"

You say, "Tito?" We hardly ever heard of Tito. We know he was a resistance fighter in the forests of Yugoslavia since 1942; and he has been trying to build up his army.

After King Alexander was assassinated in October 1934, a Serbian Nationalist, General Draza Mihaijlovic became Commander in Chief. He fought against the communist resistance fighter, Josip Broz Tito and his Partisans. It seems like Tito crawled out of the woodwork overnight. He sure hates the "Te Svabo" the (Danube Swabians), and wants Yugoslavia be rid of them."

An old man down the street muttered, "Our ancestors came here and settled in 1763 by invitation from Empress Maria Theresa of Austria and made this land productive. We lived in peace with all the people around us. We did not harm anyone and now we just have to hand everything over. We are hated since we are of German descent – all because of the crimes committed by Hitler's army. We lived in this territory 180 years and Yugoslavia just came into being since the end of WW I– this injustice – all because of Hitler."

The inhabitants of Sentiwan were stunned, "What will be next?"

The peaceful life in Sentiwan was gone. Gone....... as if it never even existed. Gone forever, never to return....ever!

It was December 27, 1944, when the town crier again summoned young men between the age of 17 and 45 and women between 17 and 30 to appear at the Sportsplatz by noon.

Everyone was under the impression that they were being sent off on yet another work assignment. When all were assembled, Russian soldiers with guns surrounded everyone and announced that they would be sent away on a work assignment. Next was an alphabetical roll call, read from a document from the town hall that listed the names of all young people who lived in Sentiwan. Every person whose name was called out had to step forward and was directed to one side.

My niece, Nandl (Brettraeger, Anna) and her husband were one of the first to step forward. There were many young women assembled who had brought along their small children. They had no one to watch them on such short notice. The Russian soldiers simply came and yanked small children away from their mothers and put them in a group by themselves. This was heartbreaking to watch. Mothers were crying because of the ruthless way their little ones were treated and children were crying out of fear, wanting their mothers comfort. It was a sad scene to see those forlorn little ones standing alone, wearing fear on their faces.

When the roll call was ended, there were two hundred young men and women named. The grandparents of the little children then were allowed to claim their little ones. But there were quite a few children who did not have grandparents; and they were at the mercy of strangers.

Next, the Partisaner separated the men from the women and each group was immediately marched away heavily guarded. Some were taken to the Jugendheim and were locked up. Others were marched to Theis's Tavern and locked up overnight in the tavern's dance hall, heavily guarded.

The next day, the town crier informed the families of those chosen to bring extra warm clothing and blankets and food for thirty days, put it all in a sack with the person's name on the sack and bring it to them. After their families had brought them their supplies, they were lined up. Then, armed Russian soldiers surrounded them and marched them to the district railroad station located in the neighboring town of Apatin.

Two locomotives each with forty cattle-cars attached were waiting to be boarded. However, the young men and women were not immediately boarded when they arrived there but were locked up in warehouses with a lot of other young folk from all over the Province of Batschka. There were 1,400 young people from our province waiting until all the ethnic German young people from all of Yugoslavia were herded together.

There was a total of 40,000 ethnic German young men and women, former outstanding citizens of Yugoslavia, that had been stripped of their citizenship and sent away, doomed to hard labor.

It was January 2, 1945, when they were sent off. There were two transports leaving that day. One left in the morning with forty cattle cars full of young people and the second transport left in the afternoon with forty cattle cars full.

Many tears were shed that day, as mothers and grandparents stood helpless, watching their children being hauled off into the unknown. Some families lost both their son and grandson. Some children were left without parents or grandparents and were at the mercy of strangers. When the cattle cars were filled, doors were locked securely and the locomotives hauled them away into the unknown.

Among the women on the train, there was a beautiful young pregnant woman from Sentiwan who was soon expecting to deliver her baby. She was forced to go even in her condition. She should not have been forced to go.

The train made very few stops for people to relieve themselves and it was very crowded. Under those conditions, women became sick and died. The young pregnant woman went into labor on the crowded train; and she and her baby died before they even reached their destination and were simply just thrown off the train. As the doors opened and the Russian soldiers threw off the dead bodies, the women on the cattle cars watched with horror when they saw hundreds of corpses strewn all along the side of the railroad tracks. They had previously been thrown off the train and were simply just left there.

It made my hair stand up in back of my neck when my niece, Nandl, told me all that happened on the train to Russia after she was released from there in 1948. She was on that train. It was learned later that the 40,000 young men and women were sent to Russia and Siberia.

During WW II, Tito of Yugoslavia made an agreement with Stalin. If Russia helped Tito regain the provinces that Yugoslavia lost when Hungary occupied them in 1941, then Tito in return would provide Russia with all the healthy young workers, (ethnic German men and women) needed for the rebuilding of war-damaged Russia.

A lot of those young folk died on their way even before they reached the border to Russia because of the unsanitary conditions in the cattle cars resulting from hardly any stops for people to relieve themselves. Many also froze to death because the cattle cars were drafty and Russia has bitter cold winters.

It took three weeks to reach their destination in Russia. They were transported to different areas in Russia and Siberia. My niece, Nandl, had to lay bricks and mix mortar. It was very heavy work for women. However, she survived; and when she was released in 1948, we hardly recognized her, she looked so bad.

There were forty-seven young women from Sentiwan between the ages of 18 and 32 who died working in the coal mines in either Anthrazit, or Charcov. A great number died because they did not have the warm clothing needed to survive the bitter winters in Siberia. Another factor was inadequate food for the hard labor they were forced to do.

The ones that became sick and thus were unable to work, were released and sent to Hof-Morschendorf Heimkehrlager in Germany (a camp set up for the sick and disabled persons released from Russia's labor camps. Those sent to Hof-Morschendorf, all arrived with severe medical problems and life-long health disabilities. Many of them were widowed because their loved ones starved to death in Tito's death camp in Gakowa.

When the Russians left with the 200 young folk from our town, Tito's Partisaner (soldiers) moved in. They were very brutal and sadistic. If one didn't move out of their way fast enough or walk fast enough, one could expect the butt of a rifle in one's ribs, stomach or head. It was nothing to see someone knocked down, beaten or kicked.

Everyone in Sentiwan owned a vineyard; and therefore everyone had barrels of wine stored in their cellar. They found out too quickly and helped themselves and became intoxicated. In their drunken state they began to rape little girls as young as five years old and women into their eighties. They didn't care how old. It was another very scary time for women.

Chapter 13
Happy New Year- 1945

It was early morning on New Years Day 1945, when I was awakened by a knock on our bedroom door. It was still dark and the children and I were sleeping. A year ago we would have been up early going from house to house wishing everybody "Happy New Year!" It was a tradition in our household, that, whoever of the children was first to wish - "Happy New Year!" - received a silver coin. There was competition between the children for that silver coin. Therefore, it was a day of early rising - but not this year. Ever since the Partisaner took over, life in Sentiwan was not the same. Christmas was not the same either with the man of the house gone and our valuables pilfered.

I hesitated to open the door because of all the bad things that had been happening. Then I heard a familiar voice, "Open up; it's me, Henrich." Immediately I opened the door and yelled to the children, "Dati is home, Dati is home. Get up!" They both came running with joy and surprise on their faces, happy to see their father home. We all embraced one another and hugged and just hugged.

We were curious as to how he got to come home when all the other men were still gone. Dati said, "Two days ago, a few Russian bombers flew over Stuhlweissenburg

(Szekesfehervar) airport and dropped some bombs. It was already dark; and when we realized what was happening, all of us on the repair crew darted as fast as we could into our foxhole.

We barely made it when dozens of bombers flew over dropping bombs continually. The bombers on the ground, parked along the airstrip, exploded and the fuel ignited and burst into flames. The heat was intense. Flames were everywhere and it felt like we were trapped in hell. It was continuous, non-stop bombing by the Russians. I thought it was the end of the world. None of us ever thought that we would come out of our foxholes alive. We were frozen in fear.

All of a sudden it stopped; and there was dead silence. We were expecting more of the same; so we waited and waited. I don't know how long. But no more droning sounds were heard.

One by one we climbed out and looked around at the damage. Flames were still burning; and we could see dead soldiers lying everywhere. We checked out the whole airport. There was absolutely no one alive. All were dead.

There was no one we could report to. So we removed our work uniform that we wore over our clothes and started for home. We walked all the way home from Stuhlweissenburg. It was a long walk -50 Km (32miles) to Sentiwan. It wasn't so bad walking that far with my three good friends; Heiser Sep, Fuderer Hans, Frank Stefan and my partner Tettman Stefan. We all made it back safely; and here I am. I'm so glad to see you all alive and well. After experiencing the bombings, I was worried about you all because Stuhlweissenburg is really not that far away. We had no idea what was happening elsewhere and how far the Russians advanced.

But what happened in town? - All those foxholes and the bullet holes in our house? The town looks so deserted. It doesn't at all feel like New Years."

The following day after Henrich had come home, he and his friends had to report to the town hall. A lady in town saw them coming home and reported them.

Henrich always dressed up when he had to go somewhere of importance. He wore a nice set of clothes and wore his good shoes. When they arrived at the town hall, Tito's Partisaner were already in control. They immediately took them prisoners and transported them to Apatin and locked them up in jail until they decided what to do with them because they were ethnic German. After a few days, they were sent to the head Labor Camp in Sombor. When they arrived there, they saw ten women from Sentiwan working in the Camp's laundry.

Henrich, Heiser Sep and Fuderer Hans were chosen to remodel Commandant Rajko's house. Rajko was the Commandant of the Labor Camp in Sombor. His house was right across the street from the entrance to the Labor Camp. Frank Stefan, who used to own a fabric and grocery store in Sentiwan, had no experience in remodeling and therefore was sent to town to help unload meat. In the process of unloading, a bone scratched his skin open and he got blood-poisoning. Medical treatment was denied to ethnic Germans after Tito revoked our citizenship. As a result, he died in the hospital in Sombor.

His wife Kati and I went to visit him at the hospital in Sombor the day before he died. There was no hope for his recovery when we went to see him. His body was brought back to Sentiwan and was buried the middle of February in 1945.

I don't know what happened to Tettman Stefan. Men in the Labor Camp in Sombor were sent here and there and everywhere – just at a moment's notice. Daily, people were sent to various places for work assignments.

After the remodeling of Rajko's house was completed, Henrich was sent back home to Sentiwan to work at Peitz Drexler Co. where all kind of fancy woodwork was manufactured – like carved furniture, spindled beds and chair legs. He was not allowed to come home at night and be with his family. All men working there had to sleep in the boy's school building located in the middle of town and were locked up every evening like prisoners. All those men were the men who had come home from various places as survivors of the Russian bombings when everyone else was killed. There were seventy-five men who had come straggling home. They had no idea what all went on in our town and that Tito's Partisaner had taken over and occupied Sentiwan. They were released and marched away on that horrible night, March 11, 1945, with a pick in hand and heavily guarded on all sides by armed Partisaner. They were led away, humiliated and treated like dangerous criminals. They were not told where they were taking them.

It was March 12, 1945, the night we had to assemble at the town square. After we were separated from our children and the elderly, the Partisaner marched us women out of town. It was 4:00 a.m. There were about 400 found fit for work. Just as the Partisaner started to march us away, my mother-in-law remembered that her two daughters, Noni (Horn Anna) and Rosi (Schneider Rosalia) didn't have their bread. They had forgotten to pack it into their rucksack when they gathered up their food items and had already gone down the street when she noticed their bread on the table. She decided to take the loaves with her and give it to them when she caught up with them at the town square.

Hurriedly walking toward us, she waved her arms frantically holding up a bundle containing the loaves of bread and yelled, "Noni, Rosi! You forgot your bread! Here's your bread!" She wanted to give it to them. One Partisaner grabbed her and pulled her into the group of us women and were about to take her along. All eyes were on my mother-in-law. Immediately all the young women yelled with one accord, "She's an old woman - she's an old woman!" At hearing everyone yell, they let her go. In all of this commotion, she did however manage to give them the bread.

We were treated like convicted criminals escorted on both sides and in rear with 30 heavily armed Partisaner. All the teary eyes of the elderly and crying children were on us, watching us leave. It was so humiliating to be led away from our families and children in such a manner - as if we had committed an awful crime.

They marched us out of town taking the road leading to Apatin on the Danube. When we arrived there, we found it odd that the gates to the houses were left open and a lot of dogs were roaming the streets. This was unusual because in all the towns in our region that were inhabited by ethnic Germans, people had the habit of closing the gate to the yard to keep dogs from roaming. One rarely saw a gate left open. We learned later on that the Partisaner had rounded up all ethnic German women from Apatin that were fit for work and took them to the Labor Camp in Sombor. This was done the day before we arrived in Apatin.

Chapter 14
Labor Camp in Sombor

The Partisaner marched us through Apatin and on to
the Labor Camp in Sombor. All that time, there were no
stops to rest. Whoever got tired and sat down was shot
and killed. Observing their brutality kept one moving no
matter what. We arrived in Sombor late afternoon at 5:00
p.m. After having marched 26 Km carrying our backpacks
of food and carrying our shovels, we were all so exhausted –
to the point of passing out. However, we were not allowed
to sit and rest when we arrived there. We had to stand up
all night long under the starry sky. We all leaned on one
another to hold each other up.

In the morning while it was still dark, we were split up
into small groups and were assigned our living quarters -
wooden barracks with straw covering the floor. The barracks
were old and infested with Wanzen (bedbugs), an insect
similar to lice only larger, which came out of the wood at
night and sucked our blood while we were sleeping.

Each of us was given a sleeping spot on the straw. At
5:00 a.m. we had to line up in groups of ten people in a row
with four rows. Then there was a big space and again ten
people in a row with four rows, and so on.

Commandant Rajko came and picked out forty women, including myself, to work in the hospital in Sombor. When the chosen forty were all lined up, the Partisaner escorted us to the hospital. There, all the wounded Russian and Serbian soldiers were cared for. We had to wash the floors in the hospital and do laundry and cook.

After a week, they sent thirty-five of the older women to work somewhere else, and left only five of us who were from Sentiwan. Among the thirty-five older women that were sent away was my aunt Drescher Gretl Bas, who had no shoes. Because when the drummer came throughout our town announcing that we had to assemble in the town square in two hours, she came out into the street, wearing only slippers. She wanted to see what the commotion was all about on the street; and a Partisaner came and dragged her along to the town square, the way she was dressed. She had been taking care of children whose parents were sent away to Russia on December 27. Therefore, the small, young children were left alone in the house, with no one to care for them.

I gave her a pair of my husband's shoes that I carried in my knapsack. I had intended to give those shoes to my husband in case I ran into him. Because when he was summoned to the town hall with his friends; he wore his good clothes and his nice shoes. Those were not comfortable for hard labor. He had no idea that he would not be allowed to go home after he reported to the town hall, nor did his friends.

The thirty-five women that left for labor assignments elsewhere were replaced by thirty women from the town of Milititsch. Their duty was to do the laundry at the hospital.

From then on, men had to wash the hospital floors. This routine went on until April 15, 1945, at which time we had to return to the Labor Camp in Sombor. We were told that all of us were permitted to return to our home town. We were all overjoyed that finally they would let us return home; so we hurried back to the Labor Camp.

With everyone returning from their assigned jobs, the Labor Camp in Sombor became overcrowded. Although the yard of the Labor Camp was huge, it was absolutely packed with people. The men were in a group on one side of the yard, heavily guarded; and the women were on the other side of the yard, heavily guarded. Things did not turn out as promised. We were not allowed to return home. What a let-down!

They took us one by one into the barracks and proceeded to take away our rings, earrings, necklaces, watches, and money if anyone happened to have some in their pockets. If they checked people that had hidden their valuables and they found them, they were brutally beaten.

While we were waiting our turn to be searched, I spotted my husband in the crowd of men also waiting to be searched. However I was not allowed to talk to him; but I was very happy to learn that he was alive. So many people had been needlessly shot, that one did not know from moment to moment who would be next. I found out sometime later on that Henrich, along with the group of seventy five men were sent to the town of Besdan which was surrounded by a big forest. There they had to cut wood for the Serbian government.

The only good thing that happened as a result of us being brought together was that we were able to find out the whereabouts of our spouses, children, and the elderly; because news from all over spread around like wild fire. That's when we also first learned about Tito's murders of thousands of Danube Swabians.

Many women there who worked in various places outside of Sombor knew me in our home town, Sentiwan. I asked several if they had any knowledge of the whereabouts of my children. A woman, who was sitting in the barracks, told me that my son Joschi, who was twelve years old, was sent to Karawukowa with a group of boys his age. There, an elderly man needed boys to tend his cows. He was good to the boys and, daily, gave them milk to drink.

At the same time I found out what had happened to the children and the elderly. I was told, that on March 12, 1945, after we were marched out of Sentiwan, the children and elderly were locked up in the Cloister School for three days and then evacuated and taken to the death camp - Gakowa. I was horrified when I heard that.

After they had robbed us of our valuables, we were again sent back to the hospital and others to their previous labor tasks.

An older man and I were given the task of cleaning the top floor of the hospital. He was washing the floor; and I did the dusting, washing windows and beds. One day while I was washing the windows, I noticed my husband in a group of laborers marching by. I banged on the window pane, but continued to wipe the window vigorously as though I was working real hard. I managed to get his attention so that he would know it was me. I noted the time in the morning when they marched by. Of course, he was the only one that looked up. Every morning at the same time I went to the window and waved to him, pretending to wipe the windows. He always looked up when they marched by and so I got a glimpse of him daily for about three weeks until he got relocated to another work duty in Esseg. Even though he could not wave back, at least I knew that he was alive.

At the hospital in Sombor, the Russian officials and the doctors had their offices on one side of the top floor; while the other side was for patients. The main floor was for patients only.

Every day the officers were served the best meals; and when their meal was ended, the food trays were placed on a long table in the hallway to be scraped off and washed. Those of us working were considered slaves and were only served pea soup daily. The food on those trays smelled so good; and we all yearned just for a morsel of some of that food. I noted the time when their meal was ended and the food trays containing still lots of food scraps on them were put on the table for cleanup. When no one was around, I sneaked up to the table grabbed a few pieces of food and hid them in my apron and dashed back to work. Later on at night, I shared some of my morsels with my friends in our sleeping quarters in the basement. Our sleeping quarters were straw-covered cement floors.

All chickens that were used to prepare the meals at the hospital were brought from our hometown, Sentiwan. There was a man named Toni, working in the hospital, who spoke the Serbian language well. He understood all that the officers were saying. He overheard them say, that, all the meat served came from Sentiwan. Toni used to tell us all kinds of news that he had overheard.

A drainage trench, leading from the kitchen to the garbage pit outside the hospital, was full of left over food scraps and the soup with meat in it flowed like a river to the garbage ditch; yet we were only served pea soup and a hunk of hard corn bread. We were yearning for some of that food; but we were denied.

The other slave women took care of the main floor. The Serbian women, who were visiting their wounded at the hospital, all wore the beautiful colored velvet and satin jackets and the long white dress shirts that they pilfered from us when their husbands searched our houses. They had pilfered our houses and took our nice clothing for their use. Even many Partisaners (soldiers) that did not have a soldier uniform wore those beautiful colored women's jackets as their jackets. We all knew where they came from because each ethnic German town had a specific code of dress.

My forced labor assignments were nearly all spent in the city of Sombor. I worked at the hospital until the end of July; when I was sent back to the Labor Camp. I was chosen to cook food for the internees and do the Partisans' laundry.

While I was working in the kitchen, I prepared a basket of food daily for Commandant Rajko and his wife and delivered it along with their laundry to their house directly across the street from the Labor Camp. This food that I took over to their house was food that had been confiscated from ethnic Germans who were brought as prisoners to the Labor Camp. Anyone that had any food with them when they were brought to the Camp had to give it up. They were then beaten and thrown into the "White House." – an old shell of a delivery truck similar to a UPS truck, painted white on the outside with a door in the front and a door in the back, no windows. It served as a prison for about ten people.

I got to know Commandant Rajko and his wife real well with this daily routine. One day I found out about my husband's illness from someone returning from their work assignment. The woman had told me that he was so sick that he was sent to Gakowa to die.

There were so many bad rumors circling about the conditions in Gakowa that I was beside myself with worry. My girl, Lisl, was always sick from the time she was born and I had no idea whether she was still alive or not. How could she be with all the bad things I had heard about the death camp. Now Henrich was also sent there.

I was so relieved to know that Joschi was all right. The constant worrying and not knowing about their welfare was wearing on my nerves. I lay awake night after night praying to God for an answer. I was rehearsing scenes in my mind on what to say and how, trying every possible way to approach Commandant Rajko for permission to let me go to Gakowa to see about my sick husband.

Commandant Rajko was an arrogant man, one that could not easily be persuaded. There was never a pleasant expression or smile seen on his face. He was even rough with his own Partisaner men.

One day I chanced it and asked him to let me go to Gakowa when he stood next to me while I dished out the soup to the slave laborers. He always stood next to me to make sure that I only put one ladle full of soup per person, no more. I felt so sorry for the men who were lined up waiting for their meal after a hard day's work. When they came near to receive their soup, they were so hungry that their hands shook and trembled. I was hoping that he would go away so that I could give those starving men two ladles full of soup. But he would not budge from the spot next to me till all were served. I just could not understand how any human being could be so cruel.

I pleaded with him to give me a pass to Gakowa just for one day to see how my husband was; but he refused with an absolute NO.

His wife was a nice lady so I toyed with the idea that maybe, just maybe, I could ask her and she in turn could influence him to let me go. I was set in my mind to ask her the following day when I took over the basket of food. When I handed her the food, I begged her to hear my request.

"Mrs. Rajko! Please, would you ask your husband to give me permission to go to Gakowa? My husband is very sick and I long to see him. Would you please? Would you?"

She looked at me with tender, sympathetic eyes, hesitated for a moment, and then replied, "I will ask him and I will let you know tomorrow, but no promises that he will let you."

I appreciated her willingness to help me and said, "Thank you! Thank you! I will see you tomorrow about this time. Thank you for your kindness!"

I was tossing and turning all night long hoping for the time to pass and for morning to break. I was hopeful that perhaps she could influence him to give me permission. The day dragged on. I could hardly wait for supper time. Carrying the food across the cobble stone street, I was hopeful. I knocked at the front door. The door slowly opened and from the saddened expression on her face, I immediately knew that my request was denied.

Mrs. Rajko said: "I am so sorry, Lisa. He told me that husband and wife of any German cannot be together. He told me to tell you an absolute "NO!"

As I set the basket containing the food on the kitchen table, she walked toward a desk, picked up a small object and came toward me handing me a small white mother of pearl covered prayer book – printed in German.

"Here, Lisa, take this little prayer book – maybe it will bring you comfort."

Very disappointed, and with an ache in my heart, I slowly reached out my hand and took hold of the prayer book, thanked her again for trying and left the house with a heavy heart. My hopes were dashed. How can anyone be so unfeeling? Could he not have a little consideration, show a little kindness, just a little bit? I became angry in my thoughts at this pompous man. I knew someday he would have to meet his maker and account for his cruel actions.

As I walked across the cobble stone street to the entrance of the Camp, I heard a loud voice shouting, "Yasam Bog!" (I'm your God!) "Go ahead and pray to your God, but it will be no use. "Yasam Bog!" – (I am your God!) – "here... things go MY way!"

I recognized the familiar voice. It was Rajko's voice. He said this to some women whom he, by surprise, caught praying behind the barracks after they had returned from their work assignments. Praying was not allowed. They were so deep in prayer that they were not aware of his presence.

As I slowly made my way back to the kitchen, my thoughts were, "Your time will come, Rajko, your time will come!"

In the stillness of the night as I lay on my straw-covered sleeping spot and with a heavy heart I poured out my soul to God. There has to be a way! I need to know how my husband is! I want to see my children! Lisl was always sick back home. Is she still alive? I must find a way....I must! "Please....Oh God....Hear my prayer...Help me."

Chapter 15
I Must Find a Way

Days passed, weeks passed, with the constant gnawing of the welfare of my loved ones on my mind. Every night I prayed to God to help me find a way.

One evening in September as a group of us were cleaning up the kitchen, we ran out of water. It was my turn that week to fetch water from the well. The well was located just outside the high barbed wire fence that surrounded the Labor Camp. One had to go past the Partisaner guarding the gate to the outside.

I picked up the water can as usual and headed outside, walking toward the gate. As I came near the well, something seemed very strange, out of the ordinary. There was absolutely no one in sight by the gate – not a guard, not a Partisaner to be seen in the whole compound, absolutely no one. At an instant I quietly put down the water can and darted out the gate and hastily made my way down the street and toward the railroad tracks. Since I was familiar with the lay-out of Sombor, I knew how to get to the railroad tracks. While I was working in the kitchen I asked numerous people if they knew how to get to Gakowa; and they all told me, "Just follow the railroad tracks. They lead right to town."

It was eighteen Kilometers to Gakowa. I had a long, painful walk ahead of me since I had been bothered with a sore cracked heel for some time. I did not have any shoes. All I owned was a pair of wooden sandals. I walked all night long just wearing wooden sandals.

Occasionally my heel slipped off the soles and dirt imbedded into the crack in my heel. When it began to dawn and the sun peeked over the horizon, I noticed that my heel was bleeding; and it was very painful. I told myself, "I have to go on. I have come a long way. I'm almost there. This is no time to give up."

It was now day break and mine eyes searched in all directions to make sure that there was no one in sight. I was glad that corn fields lined both sides of the tracks that I could hide in if perhaps I noticed someone in the distance. I decided to stay on the tracks because the ground was more even since my walk now had turned into a limp with my ailing foot.

"I must be vigilant!" I told myself. Painfully, limping along, being preoccupied with my sore heel I bent down to check the bleeding and as I straightened up, I was startled to find Straschar, Commandant Rajko's assistant standing before me. He had been to Gakowa and was on his way back to Sombor.

"Guda Idesh, Lisa?" translated, "Where are you going, Lisa?" he asked me and "who gave you permission?" I did not expect this and was at a loss for words for a second. I was groping my mind for a quick answer.

"Rajko gave me permission to see about the welfare of my sick husband" was my reply. He knew me well because of the daily trips to Commandant Rajko's house. This quick answer satisfied him and he never even asked me for my pass and walked on.

As I came closer to Gakowa, I had to sneak through the cornfields so I would not be detected; and there in the corn field I ran into my little girl. She and a few girls were playing in the corn field. When she saw me, she stopped, looking puzzled, then whispered with a quizzical face, "Mami?"

We were both so surprised to see each other. "Lisl, you're alive! I'm so glad you're alive. Thank God! But, Oh! You're so skinny, just skin and bones. And, how come you have no hair? What happened to your red hair?" We flew into each others arms and hugged. Then Lisl told me, "People came around and sheared every one because of all the lice."

We carefully sneaked out of the cornfields and into the gardens. Each house in Gakowa had a garden behind the house. The outhouse ditch was located in the garden and therefore, people all day long were seen there.

As we headed toward the living quarters, Lisl told me that Dati worked and wouldn't be home until evening. I was so happy to hear that Henrich was alive, I almost didn't believe it. I had to see him. It had been quite some time since I had found out that he was near death and that he had been taken to Gakowa. I really didn't think that he would make it, when I overheard people talking about the conditions of the death camp. I had a hard time waiting till evening. Lisl was very worried about Oma.

As we entered the room and I saw Oma lying on the straw-covered floor, all skin and bones with lice crawling all over her body from head to toe, I was shocked. I couldn't believe what I saw. She was so weak she almost couldn't acknowledge my presence.

There was so much "catching-up" to do since we last saw each other. Lisl told me that she never got sick ever since they've been placed into the concentration camp – only the big sores all over her body from malnutrition. However, the knowledge of herbs by some older women helped many to overcome their ailments.

When Henrich walked through the door that evening, Lisl said softly in excitement, "Dati is home." I turned around and was so happy to see his presence; but my heart ached when I saw how skinny he was and how pale his complexion. Then Joschi walked in after having worked in the corn fields all day. He was surprised to see me. I was overcome with emotion when I saw Joschi, my first born, coming toward me. My family was standing before me – unharmed and all still alive amidst all this misery. Thank God!

It was March 12 in Sentiwan, since the last time I had seen my family. We hugged one another. To see them all was worth the risk I took. I was so happy to be with my family, to be able to see my children and my husband after such a long, long time. We all slept together in a back room and I was glad that my escape had paid off after so many months of planning it.

However, the next day some time after Dati and Joschi had gone to work, two Partisans came storming into the house, guns in hand, looking for me. I recognized them immediately. They were the Partisaner from Sombor's labor camp, two of Rajko's comrades.

I pleaded with them to let me stay; but they yanked me away from my little girl and dragged me outside. I could not bear to see the look on my girl's face and the tears streaming down her cheeks. The pain of being separated again was unbearable. My heart was breaking. I could not swallow my tears and was led away sobbing. It was a slow, painful limp to the railroad station because my heel had developed an abscess as big as a chicken's egg.

There was no sympathy on my behalf from the two Partisans forcing me to keep moving. We boarded the train in the afternoon and about a half hour later arrived in Sombor.

That half hour train ride was the longest and most dreaded that I ever experienced. The fear of the unknown was unbearable as I was recollecting all the cruel things that Rajko allowed done to his prisoners by his Partisaner.

Most of all was the fear of being thrown into the "White House" that stood in the middle of the yard away from all buildings. It was a shell of a truck much like a UPS truck. It was painted white and served as a prison for up to ten people. It had no windows but it had a door in front and a door in the rear. All whosoever tried to escape and got caught, were beaten beyond recognition and thrown in there and locked up for several days without food or being let out to use the latrine.

For the need to relieve themselves, people had to do their business on the floor of the truck. Since there were no seats to sit on, prisoners had to either stand up or lay on the filthy floor. If someone was beaten badly and could not stand up, that person had to lie in the filth of the urine and human excrement. Since there were no windows, the stench of that truck was unbearable, especially in the summer's heat. In the winter, prisoners were not allowed to wear a coat or have a blanket. Sometimes prisoners were locked up for three days without food. When they were finally released, the people smelled so bad that one could not go near them and they had to get hosed off.

The wife of one of my husband's good friends was punished and locked up in the "White House". She lost control of her senses while she was in there; and in her rage she broke open the door and jumped out, only to get beaten some more. Then she was transferred somewhere else out of Sombor.

Any Partisan soldier in the labor camp could take any prisoner into the "White House" and act out his rage on that person in any sadistic manner he desired. People that were locked up in there for several days never really recovered health wise and often died shortly thereafter or were dead when brought out.

When the train came to a stop and we got off, fear gripped a hold of me. The worst kind of thoughts accompanied me all the way back to the Labor Camp. When we arrived, the two Partisaner who brought me back, went to the office and reported my arrival to Rajko.

He came out toward me with a dirty smile on his face, took my arm and led me to the middle of the yard. I could hardly take another step, my foot hurt so much. Then he sent his soldiers to all the barracks and ordered everyone to come out and observe.

As I saw all the people coming out of the barracks, fear took hold of me, fear that I had never known before. I started to shake. What will they do to me before they throw me into the "White House?" I thought the worst.

When everyone was assembled, Rajko walked towards me and stood next to me and yelled out, "See this is what happens when you try to escape. We'll get you and bring you back, no matter where you are – we'll find you!" After yelling that out, he dismissed his soldiers and all the people and ordered me to be taken to the "Ambulant," a sick room for people that had minor illnesses till they recovered.

No medicine was given to ethnic Germans. I was stunned. I could not believe what just happened. I did not get beaten. They didn't shoot me. They didn't throw me into the "feared" - "White House." I was in a daze. I tried to find a reason for this peculiar experience. I could not come up with a single reason. My only thoughts were that he didn't punish me because he had shown a lot of respect for Henrich when he remodeled his house.

In Yugoslavia and the surrounding countries, it is a solemn tradition to show hospitality or to honor someone as a friend by offering the person to be honored a bottle of good brandy or whiskey. First, one has to take the first sip to show that it was not harmful, then, one hands the bottle over to the person to be honored or befriended as a gift. He knew that Henrich was my husband. Henrich used to send word to me when we were still at home in Sentiwan to send him a bottle of whiskey so he could give it to Commandant Rajko. I sent a bottle of whiskey on more than one occasion to Henrich while he remodeled Rajko's house; and every time he gave it to Rajko.

We had an old friend, whom I asked to harvest the grapes of our vineyard in October 1944 in exchange for a few bottles of whiskey because we had 45 rows of grapevines. Harvesting the grapes was too much work for a woman with the men all gone to war. All we picked were the grapes that the children and I ate; and the ones we stored up in the attic for about a month's worth of eating.

I was in the "Ambulant" for two weeks trying to recover from my sore heel without any medicine. My cousin, Traub Barbara, was sent to work on a farm at that time; and in the evening when she returned to the Labor Camp brought back a ripe tomato which she had hidden in her clothes. In the evening, she came to the "Ambulant" to visit me and brought me the ripe tomato and cut it in half and placed it on the abscess on my heel and bandaged it up with rags. The next day, the abscess came to a head and broke open and all the puss ran out. I repeated the process with the other half of the tomato and soon thereafter, I was on my way to recovery. After I was released, I was put back to my former job of cooking in the kitchen.

Just before winter, I was hired out as a housekeeper by a Croatian family named Bartlitsch, who operated a grocery store at the outskirts of Sombor. They were real nice people. They even offered to harbor my little girl if Henrich could smuggle her out of the death camp; which he managed to do in late February of 1946. Lisl was able to stay with me at the Bartlitsch's for one month until the event when Rajko and his rowdy Partisaner during a drinking party dismembered a man taken from the barracks and brought to Rajko's office.

He was alive when they started to butcher him in the office. His screams of pain were heard by everyone near the Labor Camp. The slaughter of the man became known all over Sombor. There was an investigation. Rajko refused to take the blame and accused his Partisaner for the slaughter. This angered them. Therefore, the Partisaner squealed on him for taking some of the gold jewelry that was taken from us April 15, 1945. All the gold was supposed to have been handed over to the Yugoslavian government.

Commandant Rajko was convicted and sentenced for life. He was incarcerated in the OSNA, a highly guarded prison in Sombor; and a new Commandant was put in his place.

The Bartlitsche's were afraid in all this turmoil, that maybe, someone will find out that they had stashed an ethnic German child; and their lives might be in danger. I needed to think of where we could take her to be safe. My husband's aunt in Apatin came to my mind. In the early Nineteen Hundreds, she had married a Serb named Mihailowitsch who was attracted to her and the ethnic German way of life and their skills. She did not have to go into the concentration camp because she was married to a Serb. The Bartlitsche's arranged for me to take Lisl to Mihailowitsch, Nanni- neni (neni = elderly aunt), who lived in Apatin.

My brother-in-law, Schneider Franz, whose boss also harbored Franz's daughter, Lisi, gave him permission to take Lisi out of Sombor. Therefore, Franz and I took both Lisi and Lisl to live with their great-aunt Mihailowitsch Nanni-neni in Apatin using bicycles. We dropped them off and returned to Sombor the same day and thanked our employers for being so kindhearted.

The new Commandant ordered all hired out laborers to return to the Labor Camp immediately. When everyone had returned, he assigned a group of us women to work in the fields, hoeing.

Sometime in June 1946, several of us were sent to pick corn at the Juranowitsch Pusta (a big collective farm). After that, we were sent to a big estate farm outside of Sombor to hoe the corn fields. There were quite a few of us in our group; and an older Jewish man was the overseer of the work. Our sleeping quarters were in a shed, with straw covering the floor for our bed. I chose my bed of straw near the door of the shed because a plan of escape was constantly on my mind since the new Commandant didn't know us that well and would not have missed me. There were no written records kept of prisoners. The Partisaners did not know how to read or write. We were always lined up in rows of four people to a row and marched away to our jobs.

I did not confide in anyone about my plan to escape. One night as I lay there, I decided to chance it in the morning before dawn. I told myself, "This is it." I got up and carefully opened the door trying not to make any noise. I managed to sneak out without being heard and again headed in the direction toward the railroad tracks. As I started out I was so scared that I started to shake all over. I remembered the last time I escaped.

I was not familiar with the area and I was not quite sure if I headed in the right direction because it was still dark and hard to see. I was walking all alone in the dark, not knowing who I would run into, dropping down at the slightest sound. I was scared like a rabbit. My biggest fear was getting caught and thrown into the "White House," the other, coming face to face with a torture loving Partisaner.

The unknown was my biggest enemy. Trying to run till out of breath, wanting to rest but could not, because I would not make it before daylight if I did. I was pushing myself to the utmost of my abilities. There were prayers ascending to God above for strength. There were doubts... fear.... panic. My emotions were running wild. I had no idea how long it would take to reach my destination. I had stumbled upon the railroad tracks and didn't even know it. I half ran and I half walked on the tracks and wasn't even aware of it.

As it began to dawn, I found myself near the outskirts of Gakowa. I decided to sneak through the corn fields hoping to outsmart the pace of the Partisaners foot steps and not be detected. The Partisaner patrolled the outskirts of Gakowa. If one waited and counted their foot steps, one could run when they walked away and hide before they returned to their spot.

I headed toward the cemetery because there I would not be too conspicuous since a lot of grave diggers were already working there. They used a big trencher to dig the big pits for the stacked up piles of the dead. The odor of death was thick in the air. It went up my nostrils and was so strong, I became nauseous. How can one stand to smell this day after day?

It was not very pleasant, either, to walk among all the piled up corpses, lying there to be buried. There were no coffins. The dead had some very twisted expressions on their faces, some with eyes wide open, some bodies bloated and already dripping from the heat. It was an unbelievable, horrible sight – very difficult to get out of one's mind. I went to some grave diggers and asked them, "Do you know a Binder (nickname) Henrich?" "I am his wife; and I would like to find him." Then one spoke up and said, "I know him. I'll send someone to get him. Just go into the first house next to the cemetery and wait for him there. I'll tell him you're there." I said, "Dank sche!" I thanked him and headed toward the house he mentioned. I went into the house and waited. It was empty. All in there had died. I was on edge and very frightened.

When Henrich came in, I hardly recognized him. He had long hair and a beard; and his skin tone was all yellow – his face and neck and arms, a tone of yellow. I had never seen anyone with that color skin tone before. He looked so drawn.

When he came into the room, we hugged each other and he told me that he would take me to the newly established "children's home." We sneaked to the "children's home" through the gardens behind the homes in Gakowa. We got there safely; and we parted because we could not afford to be seen together. He needed to go back to the wagon repair shop.

I did see him though occasionally because one of his jobs was to make kindling and chop wood for the fire for the big cooking kettles, in which soup was cooked for the children.

This house was set aside in spring of 1946, for all the orphaned children whose grandparents had died during the previous long cold winter because they froze to death. The Serbian government decided to put all the orphans in this house and fatten them up before sending them to the Yugoslavian orphanages and raise them for their future soldiers.

I could not stay with my husband or else suspicion would have been raised and I would have been taken away. When I entered the house, my eyes circled the room, observing all the starved bodies of children lying there with labored breathing. My heart went out to these poor little ones. It was an unbelievable sight. They were all covered from head to toe with sores and scabs as a result of malnutrition; and red patches that were caused by scratching after being bitten by lice. Some were just clinging to life by their last breath. A lot of them were only covered with rags - their clothes were just plum worn out.

A feeling of sorrow and helplessness came over me. How could Tito keep this such a secret from the rest of the world and get away with it. In such a short time, so many families were wiped out. What did we do to have such injustice meted out to us?

The odor of death was sensed throughout all of Gakowa. Oh God! Please have mercy on these - little ones. My nephew Andresl (4 yrs. old) was also in the house. His mother had died of Typhoid fever in April; and I was so glad that I could take care of him. Henrich's sister, Schneider Rosi, was also in there helping to care for the children because Franzi was in there because he needed special care after a long bout with typhus. We women, fed them and washed them and oiled their sores and tried to be a comfort to them as best as we could

Even though the food was a little better, the children had been starved for so long, that it was a slow process because wholesome food was lacking. I slept in the room with Andresl and the rest of the children and cared for them for about one month; and then they were shipped away to Yugoslavian orphanages in Bosnia.

It broke my heart when my little nephew, only 4 years old was lined up on the street to be sent away and I couldn't do anything about it. They yanked him away from me; and he was crying because he wanted to stay with me; but I was not his mother. I cried so hard. I felt so helpless; but, I could not keep him.

They lined them up on the road and marched them through Gakowa to the railroad station. While they were marching, they had to sing Serbian songs which they had been taught by a Serbian teacher before they were shipped out. The words to the songs were praising Tito and his Partisaner.

They had to sing out real loud, "Drusche Tito, mladi Partisani, miwo liwo svoi rotni Kraj!" (Our friend Tito and our sweet Partisans – we'll follow on our kings road). It made me sick that they made the children sing those songs after they had killed their parents and grandparents and were planning to use them as their future soldiers.

That was sometime in August of 1946. After the children were boarded and taken away, I went throughout the house checking out the rooms. I noticed that a blanket was left behind in one of the rooms. Since I did not have a coat or a blanket, I claimed that blanket for myself.

One day late August, a drummer went throughout Gakowa announcing that the town of Bereg was looking to hire a barrel maker. Barrel makers needed to report to Commandant Schutzo.

Henrich went to Commandant Schutzo and bargained with him that the Commandant would let him take his entire family along to Bereg.

With a battle of words, Henrich's courage won. He got Schutzo's permission. The last week of August, 1946, Henrich, Joschi, and I were sent to Bereg using a horse-drawn wagon.

Part III
The Conclusion of Lisl's Story

Part III is a continuation of Part I. Lisl tells the story of her and her family's adventure of trying to go back to the land of their ancestors, Germany, after they escaped from Bereg in Yugoslavia crossing the border into Hungary on that rainy night.

Part III starts with Lisl's father asking the kind farmer, who found them in his small barn, where to go to find work.

Chapter 16
Destination Germany

My father spoke the Hungarian language fluently, so when the kind farmer returned, Dati asked him where we were. We had no idea how far we had come since we walked all night long trying to get as far away from the border as we possibly could. We had never before been in this part of Hungary.

The farmer informed us that we were just at the outskirts of Hercogszanto and the distance to Davod was about seven kilometers. Dati told him briefly about our circumstances and about our need to find work. The farmer suggested that we inquire for work at an estate farm called Bischbeck Pusta nearby. He informed us that they hired poor people and employed even families with children. While the parents worked, the children of all the families employed there played with one another till quitting time at 5:00 p.m. Food was provided for all the workers and their children.

When our clothes were dry, we thanked the farmer for his kindness and left to go to the estate farm to inquire for work. As we came close, we saw long, sectioned-off parcels of land planted with barley, beets, potatoes, and corn. The tender green plants looked so pretty in contrast with the black fertile soil.

In the distance we saw a huge mansion. Everywhere one looked; people were working, hoeing, and digging. When we arrived at the estate office, the overseer immediately hired Mami and Joschi to hoe the corn while I was taken to the yard where the children played. We were given shelter for the night in an empty Tschardach (a small barn for storing corn during winter).

Dati, however, decided he would head into Davod to find a job as a barrel maker. Farming was not his favorite thing to do. When he came into town and walked past a house, he noticed a big barrel standing in the yard. Dati turned back and walked into the yard and asked the owner if he needed help making barrels. He employed him immediately.

Dati returned to the Pusta early evening with good news – he also had a job. Every morning at dawn Mami, Joschi, and I walked to the Pusta while Dati headed off to work in Davod. At night we all returned to the Tschardach to sleep. The barn was about half hour's walk from the Pusta.

It took three weeks for us to diligently save every Forint (dollar) we received from both jobs to be able to afford a train ticket to St. Gotthardt, the border town between Hungary and Austria, and from there, on to Germany.

One day the drummer, the town crier, went throughout the streets of Davod, shouting this message, "All those who are not citizens of Hungary must leave the country!" When Dati returned to the Tschardach that night, he told Mami about the drummer's message and suggested that they count the money to see if there was enough saved for a train ticket to St. Gotthardt, the town located on the border between

Hungary and Austria. The fare was thirty Forint. With the money they would still receive, it would be sufficient.

The next day, Mami informed the owner of the Pusta of our situation. He paid her for the wages due her, plus he gave her five pounds of dry beans and a loaf of bread and bode us farewell.

Dati and Mami put their knapsacks on their back and away we went to the railroad station in Davod. Dati went to the ticket window and asked for a ticket to St. Gotthardt. The man took a ticket and with a lead pencil wrote down June 9 to St. Gotthardt. Dati gave thirty Forint to the cashier who, in turn, handed the ticket over to my dad. He put the ticket in his pocket and we proceeded to board the train.

I was all excited because it had been a long time since I rode on a train. As we stepped into the wagon, we noticed that all seats were taken. It was crowded – standing room only. I heard the conductor blow his whistle; and the wagons started to jerk and jerk. I had to hold on tightly so I wouldn't loose my balance and step on other people's toes. After a few jerks, the train rolled along smoothly.

Looking out the window, I saw the telephone poles flying by, in a rhythmic motion; and I noticed the perfectly elongated rows of the farmers' plowed fields, one green, one brown, one green, one brown, stretching out and unfolding like a giant paper fan. I was amazed at how perfectly straight those rows were planted. I was so engrossed that I did not realize that the train slowed down and came to a full stop. Time had gone by so quickly; and we were already at our first stop in Baja (Baia). The conductor had not even come by to collect our tickets.

All of a sudden the door flew open and the Hungarian border guards with guns in hand came in and yelled, "All foreigners must leave the train immediately!" making their way down the isle to check people's identification papers and passports. They went from wagon to wagon. Since we did not have any papers, we had to get off.

It was noon when we arrived in Baja. One hundred people were rounded up; and we were taken to the barracks of the border guards.

The barracks were located close to the train station. When we entered the barracks, we noticed that there were already a few hundred foreigners inside. Everywhere I looked, I saw worried faces; and from every direction in the room, all kinds of questions were heard. "What's going to happen to us?" "Where will they take us?" People were nervous, pacing back and forth, biting nails, sighing, moaning. The unknown was the worst part of the wait.

When it got dark, about 8:00 p.m., the Hungarian Schandar (soldiers) arrived. They were heavily armed. They lined us up outside the barracks and escorted us away. There were a few hundred people in a column surrounded by armed soldiers. It was dark. We could not see where they were leading us. We were not familiar with that part of the country.

As we were walking along, I became very hungry. My stomach growled; and I wished I had a piece of bread. The longer we walked, the hungrier I got. Along side my family there marched a Schandar who had a friendly nature. I was sooo hungry I mustered enough courage that I walked over to him grabbed him by the hand, pulled on his fingers to get his attention and asked, "Batschi! Gerem seben,

ganjer?" Sir, do you have a piece of bread?" "I'm so hungry."
He replied, "I'm so sorry, but I do not have anything to eat,
if I did I would give you some."

It started to rain. We did not have anything to protect
us from getting wet. We marched on. The rain increased and
turned into a steady shower; and we were getting soaked to
the bone. I was getting tired. We had left the Tschardach
this morning before dawn to catch the train and now it was
almost 11:00 p.m. I overheard the Schandar (Hungarian
soldier) walking next to us tell the time because I could
understand the Hungarian language.

My feet ached and my wooden shoes filled with water.
On top of it, I was getting chilled. While we were walking,
many horror stories of what had happened to so many
people in the past two years were circling around, falling
on my ears. Stories of how groups of people were marched
away during the night by the Partisans, who led them to
a field near a big pit, made them undress, beat them with
barbed wire, shot them and pushed them into the pit to
die. I clutched on to Dati's hands. Fear overcame me. "Are
they planning to do this to us?" raced through my mind.
"Oh God, please don't let this happen to us."

All of a sudden, the Schandars leading us stopped and
told us that we were at the border line near Stanischitz,
Yugoslavia. That was real close to Gakowa. They told us
that they were handing us over to the Partisans who in turn
would march us back to Gakowa.

Fear gripped the people. Everyone was crushed. Dati
told our family to hold on to each other and not let go
under any circumstances. Then all the Schandars made a
move and walked back and stood behind the column of

people and with one accord started to shoot their guns into the air, to signal the Partisan border guards that a group of prisoners was at the border ready to be handed over. I was terrified at the sound of the guns all going off at the same time. I thought that they were going to shoot us.

The Partisans across the border in Yugoslavia screamed at us, "Begei!.... Napolje Schwaba...Nema Leba Schwaba!" Translated means "Away with you, get out of here – there will be no more bread for you Swabians." Then they started to shoot at us because they didn't want us; and in turn, the Schandars started to shoot behind us to make us go back to Yugoslavia.

As soon as we heard gunfire, we dropped down clutching our hands tightly to hold on to one another. Ducking down, we ran sideways to our left and then ran low to the ground with all our might as fast as we could to get out of the line of gun fire.

There were so many people running every which way. There was such confusion – crying, screaming, and moaning. Hundreds of shots were fired while we were running; and soon the sound of the shots faded in the distance. In our attempt to get away, there was no time to look back. We had no idea who got shot. We were so thankful to God that we came out of this alive and that the four of us were together. "Thank God!"

We had to catch our breath and so we slowed down; but we had to go on. We had to get away from the border. Heading back to where we came from would keep us in Hungary. We walked for hours before we stumbled upon a little hut. We went inside to get out of the pouring rain and sat down on a pile of straw. Mami took off her knapsack and put it on the straw and sat on it. We were all so exhausted. I let my body drop backwards into the soft straw and immediately I dozed off.

In the morning we were awakened by the sound of a wagon rolling along. The farmer who owned the hut came in to start his chores for the day and found us all soaking wet. He was real nice and started to build a fire to help us dry our clothes somewhat. Dati pleaded with him to show us the road that would lead us to the spot where we had to cross the Danube River in order to reach St. Gotthardt. Since we weren't citizens of Hungary, we had to leave the country. The farmer lifted me onto his wagon and took us to that road. After we got off the wagon, we thanked him kindly.

As we were walking along on the road, some people came walking behind us and caught up with us. We looked and could hardly believe our eyes. It was Dati's good friend, Fuderer Hans, his wife Kati-Bas, and their two sons, Sepi and Hans. We were happy to see them. They also were on their way to Austria therefore the men decided that we go together.

We walked all day long without food; and in the evening we arrived at Dunasertsch, located on the Danube. A very nice man offered to take us across the Danube in his tschinagl (long channel rowboat). It was a very rough ride; and Mami looked scared. She was sure we'd all drown before we made it across; but we made it - all eight of us.

When we reached the other side, it was dusk. In the distance we spotted a little hut. We went to investigate and found it empty and decided to use it as shelter for the night. It was so small, that when the eight of us lay side by side, our bodies touched wall to wall; but it was still better than having to sleep in the open. We were all so very tired and had no trouble falling asleep.

In the morning we rose and resumed our journey. We had no food except our five pounds of dry beans. As we were walking along on the road, a man came walking toward us and asked if we would be interested in helping him tie up his grapevines in his vineyard. It was a three-day job with free room and board. Since none of us had any money or food, it was an offer we could not refuse. We accepted and had good food for three days. When the job was completed, we moved on in the direction of Badaszek.

On our way toward Badaszek, we came to a small town which was a Lutheran Community. They offered us a job to help them bring in the wheat harvest and gave us shelter in an empty cattle stall. We were there eight days living in the cattle stall, but were unable to work in the field because it rained every day.

All we had for food was five pounds of dry beans which Mami cooked daily until they ran out. I was so hungry that when Mami suggested I go begging for food from house to house, I did not hesitate much. When people looked at my scrawny body, they felt sorry for me. I would just ask, "Please could you spare a piece of bread for me, I'm so hungry?" Then I would receive a piece, sometimes a whole loaf or a potato or five potatoes. Sometimes they would have me come in and gave me a glass of milk. I managed to bring a little bit back to my family so we could share a little something with everyone.

The rain did not quit and it took another week for the wheat to ripen; and we had exhausted our food. We had to move on. No work, no pay.

Dati was pondering on what to do and where to go next. Absentmindedly he was fumbling in his coat pocket and felt something. He pulled it out of his pocket and saw that it was the train ticket he had purchased in Davod. They threw us off the train before the controller came by to punch and collect the tickets. It was marked June 9, St. Gotthardt. Tomorrow was June 19. A bright idea popped into his head. He had to give it a try.

The Fuderer family had no money to buy a train ticket; and Dati had an old ticket but it could be altered by simply putting the number one in front of the nine because it was written in pencil and tomorrow was June 19. All we needed was money for one train ticket for the Fuderer family.

Dati had one precious item in his knapsack – his mother's beautiful black cashmere triangle shawl with fringes all around.

After Oma had died, Dati took it out of her knapsack and put it in his. It was the shawl that she had saved for the winter ahead; but she died in October of 1945. He told Mami that he would go to Badaszek to the market and hopefully be able to sell it and get enough money for a train ticket.

He and Hans-Vetter went to Badaszek early next morning while we waited for their return in the cattle stall. A few hours later, they returned with smiling faces counting out the money. Dati sold the shawl for thirty Forint, plus a beautiful little diamond included.

Dati said, "Kindi, when we get to Germany and you get a little older, I'll have a ring made for you with this diamond in it." The diamond sparkled so pretty when sunlight touched it. I was so happy that someday in the future I would be wearing it on my finger.

Everyone put their knapsack on their back and away we went, saying good bye to the farmer and thanking him for the use of the cattle stall.

The railroad tracks coming to town ran along the out skirts of the small town near the cattle stall where we stayed. We followed the tracks to a train watch-box, a small hut that signaled the location of the train station just a little ways outside of town. The train would slow down when it came near the train watch-box; and if there were people standing to catch a ride it would stop and pick them up. But if there was no one around, the train then would resume its normal speed. One could not buy a ticket there. Tickets could only be bought at a main railroad station.

As we followed the tracks to the station, the train came by before we reached the watch-box. After it slowed down to pick up passengers and slowly started up again we ran with all our might, jumped on the train holding on to the outside handle bars, pulled us up on the platform and rode that way to Dombovar.

Dati gave Fuderer Hansvetter thirty Forint so he could buy a train ticket because they didn't have any money and we were good friends. His reason was that they had made a pact to travel together. After all, Dati had a ticket to St. Gotthardt which he intended to alter a little by placing the number one in front of the nine to make it 19 since it was written in pencil. After all Dati originally had paid for the ticket and we never rode to the end because they threw us off the train because we were not citizens of Hungary. Dati said, "I have to try it, all they can do is to throw us off again."

Hansvetter went and bought a ticket and when we attempted to board the train, they would not permit us to go on the passenger train but led us to the cattle wagon attached to the passenger cars in back because our clothes were ragged and worn.

We boarded the cattle wagon and went to one corner and we all sat down on the floor. A lot of people came on board and also sat down on the floor till the wagon was full. They were all foreigners intending to go to Austria.

Soon the locomotive started to huff and puff. I heard the whistle blowing and felt the cars jerking and in a little bit we sped away smoothly. Not long thereafter, the conductor came and started to check and collect the tickets. He made his way through the crowd sitting on the floor; and when he reached our spot, Dati handed him our ticket. He looked at us and then he studied the ticket. He looked at us again and, again, he studied the ticket.

I started to get butterflies in my stomach. "Was this a repeat of the last time we were thrown off the train?" were my thoughts. All of a sudden he put the ticket in his pocket, turned around and left the wagon. "Whew! That was close. What a relief."

There were no windows on the cattle wagon that I could have looked out and entertained myself with the scenery. So I studied the various people all around us. We were all in the same boat. Short, small, young, old, skinny, tall, wearing clothes that were ragged and worn.

It was late afternoon when we finally arrived in St. Gotthardt. Every single person had to get off the train and go to customs to have all Hungarian currency changed over to the Austrian currency before moving on. There was a huge line of people to get their money exchanged. We told them we did not have any money; and when they searched us and found none, we were taken to a place out in the open and saw other people already sitting there.

We could not cross at the border because we did not have any passports. Someone told us to take a certain road that would bypass the border guards and lead us problem free into Austria. The people we saw already sitting were waiting till it got dark to do just that.

There were a lot of people waiting that used to live in Stanischitz, Yugoslavia. They had a lot of baggage. Because when part of Hungary was awarded to Yugoslavia in 1918, half of their farms were located in Yugoslavia and the other half in Hungary.

When trouble started with Tito against the ethnic Germans in Yugoslavia, they moved their possessions to Hungary. But because all of their property was not in Hungary, they were not considered citizens and had to leave the country.

There were men near the border who made a lot of profit by helping foreigners to escape into Austria illegally. They were called Nosatsch. They would offer to carry the baggage and take people across the border for a certain fee. They waited until dark to make their move. They divided people into groups; and each Nosatsch took a group of people and told them to follow him along the border and through the woods, holding hands so no one would get lost.

We did not have any baggage or money, so we could not hire a Nosatsch. We followed them at a distance through the woods listening to the sounds they made. All eight of us were holding hands so we would not separate and lose each other.

Sometimes people fell down and let go of their clasp when they fell and became separated. We could hear people calling, "Where are you, so and so......"I'm over here!" Then we could hear people endlessly calling someone's name; but there was no response. It turned out that a lot of Nosatsches took off with people's belongings and left the people empty handed when they reached the border. The honest ones led people across and told them, "Now you are in Austria." Often people that had a lot of goods exchanged those as pay for leading them safely across the border.

After having walked all night long through mountainous forests, we found ourselves alone, just the eight of us, on a small trail leading down to a valley. We had crossed the border and didn't even know it. In the distance, as we descended, we saw a small town, nestled in the valley. We reached Weiden in Burgenland, Austria at 7:00 a.m. The sun was shining. God's splendor surrounded us. What a beautiful sight. We were free.

When we reached the valley, the road forked - one leading into Weiden some distance away and the other one leading to Schlaining which was a lot closer. So we took the road into Schlaining.

Our eyes were drawn upward to a spectacular sight. On top of a very high hill, stood a beautiful castle. It was called Burg Schlaining. It immediately drew me into the Land of Fairy Tales.

When we inquired about work, the people in town told us to go to the castle. It offered a job opportunity plus shelter.

Climbing up the steep hill took every bit of energy we had left. Our muscles ached, we were out of breath and we had to stop a few times and rest before we finally reached the top. Walking through the heavy wooden gates brought me to the land of Knights and Damsels.

We entered a large room which served as the "Office." A heavy wooden desk had been placed in front of the rear wall. The manager, a lady from Austria, sat behind the desk. She greeted us and welcomed us.

Dati and Hans-Vetter applied for a job. She explained that they were looking for men to work in the coal mine and they were required to get a physical examination to make sure they were physically fit before they could start to work. This would take a few days. Then she registered us and wrote our names in a big book. After she had all of our credentials, she left and shortly thereafter returned with blankets and took us to our new living quarters. We had to climb a lot of stairs.

We entered a very large room and it was shared with a large number of refugees. What impressed me the most about this room was a very strange kind of writing on the walls with signatures underneath – writing such as I had never seen before. I wanted to know what that was; and I was told that it was Hebrew writing. Looking out the window drew one's sight one hundred feet down to the ground below – no one could have escaped jumping out the window without bodily harm.

While we were getting settled in and Mami and Kati Bas got acquainted with our room mates, I was given a tour of the castle by older children who had been there quite some time because their fathers had been given a job in the coal mine. I was amazed looking at the very high tower at one end of the castle. They took me inside the tower. As we climbed up the spiral steps all the way to the top, I was reminded of the fairy tale "Rapunzel" and her long golden hair, - the story that my Oma used to tell me back home in Sentiwan.

When we reached the top, there stood a huge guillotine with a very sharp heavy blade resting over a big round smooth stone. Stories were told that queens and princess' heads were chopped off with that guillotine. The thought made goose bumps crawl up and down my spine. That room had an eerie feel to it; and it was not my favorite room.

We descended shortly thereafter to explore the rest of the castle. We stayed there eight days and during that time I let my imagination run wild. Someone there gave me a big book with color pictures of the "ABC" and taught me to read those letters. I had never been to school before because when the Russian soldiers occupied our town in November, 1944 all schools in Sentiwan were shut down. Then we were expelled from our homes in March, 1945. I only attended Kindergarten once in a while in Sentiwan; because I was sick a lot when I was little. I really enjoyed that book.

Since Dati was not employed yet, we did not have any food. There was no other option than for me to go begging. Since I was all skin and bones and sickly looking as a result of the concentration camp, people did not refuse me. My brother, Joschi, went with me to help me carry the gifts of food that I received. I used to go up to the door of a house and knock while my brother stayed back. When they opened the door I would ask, "Please can you spare a piece of bread, I am very hungry?" Looking at me they felt sorry for me and invited me in and gave me bread and butter and a glass of milk. Since I was really very hungry and watching me gobbled it down made their heart melt. They were very generous in their gifts of food. Times were bad after the war and people did not have all that much to spare but people shared what they could. There are kindhearted people everywhere. Sometimes I would get just a piece of bread, sometimes a loaf, or one potato. Some folks asked me if I had any brothers or sisters; and when I told them I had a brother, then they would give me more to take home. I went begging a lot in Schlaining while we stayed at the castle.

Finally the day came when the men were called into the office and were told that they were hired. They went to the mine and were given a helmet and uniforms to wear; and then they took them to the entrance of the coal mine. When Dati went to the opening of the mine and was told to go down, he stared down the endless black hole, hesitating. He just stood there and stared. All of a sudden he turned around and said to Hans-Vetter, "I'm not going down there, there have to be other jobs to be had. Let's move on." The men went to the office and told the manager that they changed their mind and that we'd be moving on. The lady reminded them to return the blankets upon leaving. We returned the blankets, thanked the lady and left the castle.

Chapter 17
Stefans Hof

After we left the castle, we just followed the road. We did not have a map and we had no idea where we were going. All I remember we went uphill and downhill, uphill and down hill all morning long. The sun was shining and it was getting hotter toward the afternoon draining every bit of our energy. We were the only ones walking on the road. Going down hill was easy; but when the road ascended, we labored just to take another step. Without food and water it was a challenge. I was so tired of walking.

It was already mid afternoon when an automobile pulled up along side of us and stopped. The officer in the vehicle asked if we'd be interested in field work. He needed workers to plow and hoe the fields. The men replied, "Surely" "Yes, Yes!" Immediately he opened the door and all of us piled in. He shifted gear and drove on toward an estate farm called Stefans Hof. This was my first ride in an automobile. It was so good to sit and rest our feet.

When we arrived, we were provided with a room that had its own kitchen. We were given food cards with which we could buy our own food. Now we were able to cook and bake our own bread again. Since we were newcomers, we were invited for an evening meal joining all workers without families. We were seated in a big dining room; and each of us was given a bowl of milk soup ("May Suppn") It was a soup made by sautéing flour in butter till lightly brown and then milk was added to make a thick broth. It looked like white flour soup. It was unique. All of us finally had a place of our own that we shared for two months. The men were given their separate jobs.

Dati was provided with a horse and plow and had to plow the fields. His horse was so old that it could not stand up on its own strength after it lay down. Every morning, Hans Vetter and Dati had to help the horse stand up by sliding a pole underneath the horse and then each going to the end of the pole lifting up with all their might. Once it stood up, it was fine and pulled the plow without any problems. That was a new experience for Dati.

Hans-Vetter was in charge of watching the apple orchard so that no one came and stole the apples before they were harvested. Mami and Kati-Bas and the boys had to hoe the fields. Every other week Mami worked and Kati-Bas kept an eye on me and cooked; and when Kati-Bas worked, Mami kept an eye on me and cooked.

Our families were paid well and continued to receive food cards. With those cards we could walk to the store in Weiden, Austria, and buy a certain amount of different varieties of food, like milk, flour, bread, butter, cheese, eggs, and cook ourselves for the first time in many months.

Dati even bought a little piglet and built a stall for it so that we could have our own meat.

Burgenland, the province where Stefans Hof was located, was very hilly country. The big farm house and office were in the valley and the fields were way up hill.

When we went shopping, we had to do a lot of lugging to get the groceries up the steep hill to our living quarters.

In the mornings, after a good rain, women and children went into the woods hunting for mushrooms. We used to bring back huge baskets full of all kinds of mushrooms. My favorite ones to gather were the Chanterelles and the big Bolete. The women cleaned them and lay them out to dry. It was a big job getting them all put up. I really enjoyed our stay at Stefans Hof. There were so many interesting things to do there; and there were so many beautiful wildflowers blooming all over.

I remember one day I needed to go to the outhouse and someone had messed on the rim. I came out of there all disgusted and ran into the lady that was in charge of cooking the meals for the workers. She asked me what was wrong and I complained about the condition of the toilet rim. She went inside the house and got a large piece of paper and a fat lead pencil and told me to write the following message she scribbled in the dirt on it and thumb tacked it to the inside of the door of the outhouse. It read: "Liebe Herrn und Damen, scheisst nicht auf den Ramen, scheisst nur in die Mitte, dass ist meine Bitte." Translated it means, "Dear Ladies and Gentlemen, don't poop on the rim, aim for the middle, that's asking very little." It solved the problem as long as we were there.

Stefans Hof was located in the Russian Zone of Austria. After WW II, Austria was divided into four zones: Russian, French, English and American. We really didn't want to stay in the Russian Zone; we wanted to move into the English Zone. But because we didn't have any Identification papers, it was hard to get a job.

Working temporarily at Stefans Hof gave us the opportunity to get a four-language passport. Dati and Hansvetter went to the town of Rechnitz to apply for passports and were told that they would be ready in about two months. We diligently saved all we could so we would be able to travel into the English Zone when the passports were ready.

It was sometime in August when the wheat was ready to be harvested.

After the wheat was in, the owner of the estate farm gave a big Harvest Thanksgiving Feast. All the farmers in the surrounding area did the same thing and joined together for celebration in the nearby town. The feast was held in a meadow just outside a small town.

Getting ready for this feast was so much fun, I still remember it to this day. The children were sent to gather red poppies, blue bachelor buttons, daisies, and other wild flowers and bring back as many as we could find. When we returned, all the horses were brushed to a satiny shine including their manes and tails. Then we braided the manes and intertwined the wild flowers as we braided. Next we tucked wild flowers into the harnesses and halters. Then the men hitched the horses to the wagons and all the farm wagons were lined up in a row all decorated.

We had a lot of fun that day. Mothers called us in to get cleaned up; and when we were all ready, the workers and their families hopped on the wagons, almost like going on a hayride, and away we went, towards town. As soon as the horses started up, everyone started to sing, everyone on all the wagons, until we reached the town. It was a beautiful sound and a beautiful sight. Everyone was happy.

When we reached the big meadow, the horses stopped and every one jumped off the wagons and headed in the direction of the tables. There were a lot of tables laden with lots and lots of delicious food.

The owner of Stefans Hof made a short speech to start the annual Harvest Thanksgiving celebration and that was followed by a prayer of thanksgiving. Then everyone could just help themselves with whatever food one desired. The town band was playing and entertained everyone until midnight. I kept sampling the food all night long.

At midnight, everyone hopped back on the wagons and when the horses started up, everyone again started to sing and we sang all the way back to Stefans Hof. It was a very special happy time for me. All that delicious food after two years of starvation made it a real feast of Thanksgiving.

Sometime after the harvest, our families decided it was time for us to leave. Dati and Hans-Vetter went to Rechnitz to pick up the passports and Mami and Kati-Bas went to Weiden to purchase a few needed items for our journey. The owner of the store, a nice lady, gave Mami a gray wool jacket to wear. It was a present from her because she felt sorry for Mami because Mami didn't even own a sweater for when the weather was cool.

When everyone got back, Dati killed the pig and Mami roasted some of it and with the rest cooked Gulash. Then we had a good supper eating Gulash; and what was left we took to our neighbors and told them not to mention to anyone that we were leaving. Mami packed up the meat she had roasted, and put it in the knapsack for food on our journey. We went early to bed that night because the plan was to leave during the night.

At 3:00 a.m. we got up, got dressed and crawled out the back window so no one would see us leave. We did not want any problems with them letting us go. The owner paid our family after the harvest was done and he was hoping that we would stay on. We did not say one way or the other; but amongst us, we wanted to leave to get into the English Zone. Stefan's Hof was in the Russian Zone. We felt it was safer there after all we went through in Yugoslavia.

We walked on the road from 3:00 a.m. till morning and from morning till almost evening - up hill, down hill, up hill, down hill. Burgenland, Austria has beautiful scenic landscapes but is very mountainous. I was so sick of walking; I started to hate the mountains. It was so tiring.

Finally as we started to go downhill we saw a farm house with a huge wagon port attached to the house where the farmer could pull his wagon under cover for the night. The farmer was busy getting his wagon ready for the next morning when he spotted us coming down the hill. He walked toward us and asked if in the morning we could help him push the wagon carrying the water up on the hill. His farm was on the hill and he wanted to take water to his workers. He was short of men. When the men agreed to stay overnight, he brought fresh straw into the breezeway for us to sleep on.

The next morning, the men helped fill the water barrels that were on the wagon and then the farmer put me on the wagon so that I didn't have to walk uphill. I really appreciated that and thanked him. He signaled the horse to start up while everyone else had to push the wagon to help make it up the hill. It was too difficult for the horse alone to pull the wagon up the hill. When we reached his field and apple orchard, the men had to help with watering while the rest of us helped pick up apples that had fallen off the trees. He used the fallen apples to make Apfel Most (Most is the German name for cider). We helped him; and at 11:00 a.m. we were all done.

While we stayed with him we told him about us wanting to get into the English Zone. He said, "Don't worry, I'll help you. Someone will take you across the border at noon." He gave all of us a glass of "Apfel Most" (apple cider). It tasted good; but we felt a little tipsy after we drank it. We never had anything like that to drink before and we had to sit down to rest.

Around noon a young lad about eleven years old arrived and told us to follow him at a distance. There was a little meadow just past the apple orchard; and the young lad led us across the meadow until we came upon a narrow brook with a little bridge over the brook. He stopped at the little bridge and motioned for us to cross it and said, "Nar schnell, nar schnell! Dann seit ihr in der Englischen Zone." Translated means "Hurry across; the English Zone is on the other side." "Hurry before the border guard comes back this way." We hurried across and after we reached the other side we turned around to thank him; but when we turned around, he was nowhere to be seen. He had told us the railroad station was near by and we couldn't miss it if we followed his directions. He had told us to go straight through the valley and at the end of the valley was the railroad station; and so it was - Fuerstenfeld Railroad Station.

When we arrived there, we parted with the Fuderer family. They had relatives in Karlsfeld, Germany, they wanted to visit. We wanted to visit Dati's sister, Horn Noni and her son, Karl in Bad Toelz; and that took us in two different directions. We knew the time would come when we had to part. We had some good times together; but this was it. We hugged and said, "Auf Wiederseh'n." and parted. I was sad to see them leave.

Dati bought a ticket and we boarded the train and rode all the way across Austria to Bischofshofen. It was located near the border to Germany. When we got off the train, the Border Patrol came and checked our passports and informed us that they were not valid in the English Zone of Austria. Our passports were only valid in the Russian Zone. Therefore, we could not go to Germany. They took away our passports and told us that we had to go back to where we came.

We were crushed. We all sat down on a bench and pondered what we could do. We had spent our money buying the train ticket; and our food was nearly gone.

Close to the station was an Inn. As Dati stared into the distance, he spotted the Inn. Dati decided to go in there and maybe get some directions on how to get to Germany. A lady, the owner of the Inn, was serving supper to her customers. Dati mentioned to her our run-in with the Border Patrol and offered her a pack of cigarettes for information on how to get to the border because the Border Patrol told us we had to go back to where we came from.

She told Dati, "Don't worry about having to go back, just take your family and go up my hay loft, spend the night, and early tomorrow morning follow the directions I'm giving you. There are quite a few people already up there who will be leaving during the night, but wait until early morning." Dati thanked her and gave her a pack of cigarettes and came out toward the bench, where Mami, Joschi and I were sitting, waiting.

He proceeded to tell Mami what the lady told him; and we were relieved that we found someone helpful who aided us on our journey. So, up the hay loft we went. When we got up there, there were already about twenty five people sleeping. We bedded down in the straw and fell asleep. At 3:00 a.m. we woke up, hearing all kinds of commotion as people were getting ready to descend the ladder. They were talking about trying to cross the border during the night to avoid the Border Patrol. They assured Dati that they knew the way. On hearing this, Dati decided to join up with them. One by one we descended the ladder, left the barn, and followed the leader, the four of us holding hands because it was dark.

We had walked quite a distance, when we came to a spot where the road forked. Dati wanted to go straight ahead according to the directions of the inn keeper; but the group insisted, they knew the way and we needed to hold to the left; so as not to argue, we followed. We walked quite some distance, all of a sudden the path ended. It was dark and hard to see which direction to go. There was no place that we could see to go, but up or back. The group insisted that Germany was over the other side of the mountain. Everybody started climbing uphill. It was a long way up to the top. Now what? There was nothing left but to go down. Because it was dark and we could not see where we were stepping, we often slid and fell. We tried to hold hands; but it was hard to do. Sometimes Dati slipped and dragged all of us down. Sometimes Mami slipped and pulled us in another direction. It was scary. Sometimes we got hung up in the brush while we were sliding and got poked with twigs and had our hands and legs scratched up. We tripped and fell and stumbled and tumbled down the mountain. Often we made a step and the rocks started sliding and tumbling down and unwillingly we followed. This went on for quite a while, I don't know how long. But when it began to dawn, it got even more frightful, because we could see how far it was down from where we were standing. When the sun finally came up, we found ourselves at the bottom of the mountain all bruised and scratched up, but nothing broken. We brushed ourselves off and looked around to get our bearings. To our surprise, we found ourselves not too far off from where we had departed. We met up with my mother's cousin Adam, his wife Evi and Seppi their baby boy. They were walking along on the road; but we could not join them because they were dressed nicely and our clothes were ragged. Adam's sister had married a Hungarian man; and therefore she did not have to go into a concentration camp. She gave them clothes after they escaped. We dared not get spotted by the Border Patrol. The Border Patrol drove back and forth on the road next to the river Salzach to keep people from illegally entering Germany.

When we worked at Stefans Hof we worked two months and diligently saved up every penny so we each could have a passport and be able to buy our train tickets. We did not intend to do it illegally; but if we went back, we could never have gotten out of the Russian Zone. One needed identification papers to get a job in the English Zone and the Passports we obtained in the Russian Zone were not valid in the English Zone. Everything we attempted did not work. One couldn't get a job without proper ID and it cost money to obtain the proper ID. So what does one do? The state of Yugoslavia uprooted us by taking away our citizenship and all whatever we owned, our homes, our land, our all. We became a people without a country. We escaped into Hungary and they didn't want us; so we escaped into Austria. But Stefan's Hof in Austria was in the Russian Zone. We were afraid to be under the control of Russia because of how we were treated when Russia occupied our hometown, Sentiwan. We had to try to get into Germany from where our ancestors originally had come; and hopefully would be accepted there.

Since we had to avoid the Border Patrol, we took the path that ran along the edge of the woods next to the River Salzach. Every time the Border Patrol drove by, we ducked down behind some brush until they were gone, and then resumed our walk.

After walking a little while, we came to a train watch-box that was located about a 15 minute walk from the main train station in Bischofshofen. The train watch-box had an office for the person in charge whose responsibility it was to flag down the train if there was trouble or if people needed a ride to the train station. There was a lady in charge at this watch-box. When she saw us coming, she came out to greet us. After talking to us, Dati mentioned to her all the problems we had encountered. She was very nice to us and invited us to come inside and asked if we were hungry. Mami told her that we already had used up the food she packed when we left Stefans Hof. While we were talking, she filled up a pot with potatoes, put them on the stove and boiled them for us. When they were done, she set them on the table and said, "Go ahead, eat!" We did not hesitate. They were delicious. While we were eating, she said, "I'll put your knapsacks on a wheelbarrow and push them to the main railroad station in Bischofshofen and give it to my brother-in-law who works there. He will put them on the train. Just stand nearby at a distance and keep an eye on him; and when he raises the flag to signal the train to depart, hurry and get on board." We thanked her for all her kindness and gave her our knapsacks; and she put them on the wheelbarrow. She said, "Give me a head start and follow me at a distance so it doesn't look like you're with me. We gave her quite ahead start when we proceeded to follow her. It was a good fifteen minute walk. After our knapsacks were placed on the train, Dati gave her one hundred cigarettes and thanked her again; and we all did from the bottom of our hearts. Then she left to go back to her duties.

As soon as our eyes detected the flag being raised, Dati grabbed my hand and we hurried to jump on the already slow moving train. Whew! We made it. The destination was Salzburg. After we caught our breath, we opened the door to the passenger wagon and attempted to take a seat. A loud voice, from a woman wearing a hat and a beautiful dress pointed toward us, yelling, "Da hast das G'sindl. Die kommen und essen uns alles weg. Die soll man vom Zug raus schmeissen. An der naechsten Haltestelle zeig ich sie an." Translated:

"Here comes more trash, just look at them, dressed in rags. They're coming into our country and are taking away our already scarce food. They should be thrown off the train. At the next stop, I'm going to report them to the authorities!" All eyes of the passengers were on us. I felt a big lump in my throat. I tried to swallow my tears, but could not keep the tears from rolling down my cheeks. I felt like crawling into a hole, I was so embarrassed and hurt. I looked at Mami and she was crying too; and that hurt me even more. The lady sitting next to her, also wearing a hat said to her, "Calm down. Don't be like that. They're human beings just like us. They're trying to survive as best as they can in these hard times." I dreaded to think what would happen to us at the next stop. It wasn't our fault that we looked so ragged. Back in our hometown we had a nice house and nice clothing. It was taken away in a blink of an eye. What would they have looked like if they were hauled away in their dresses and hats and made to live in filth for two years without soap? Since the time we escaped into Hungary, Dati, Mami, and Joschi have done nothing but work from morning till night, saving every penny we possibly could to be able to come this far, working only for food and lodging. Jobs were scarce after the war; and clothing was too expensive to buy. I mostly went barefoot because I had outgrown my shoes. In fact Dati wore two different shoes on his feet because one wore out and he found one to replace the one that wore out. Mami also wore shoes that did not fit – one shoe was bigger than the other one. I know we looked a sight; but what is one to do? Except to Thank God! that we were alive and our family was together, and hope for better times ahead.

When the train slowed down at the next station, "Salzburg," and the ladies rose to leave the train, my heart started to pump real fast. I dreaded the unknown ahead. When the train came to a full stop, every one went in file to leave the train. As we stepped down, we saw a man waving to us and motioned for us to come to him. I thought the worst. But, when we came to where he stood, he told us that he was from the Christian Center for Displaced Persons; and that he came to rescue us and provide us with shelter and food if we followed him.

"Thank You God! For your care!" were our thoughts.

We followed the man and came to a big compound of barracks. It was the Christian Center for Displaced Persons. When we arrived there, they informed us that we had to get deloused before we were given living quarters. There were already quite a lot of people there waiting to get sprayed. Men had to go to the debugging room first while the women went to get ready. We had to take all of our clothes off to our bare bottoms and hand them over to the person in charge who took them to a room with extreme heat to kill any bug that might have taken up residence. Then all the women and girls had to line up in a single row and a person in charge came with this huge dusting machine and each person got a big puff of DDT sprayed on them front and back. I was so embarrassed having to stand there in my bare bottoms waiting my turn to get dusted. I had never before been exposed or had seen anyone else, ever, without their clothes. It was the biggest shock of my life. I was relieved when we were handed our sterile clothes and finally were able to get dressed.

Next we were taken to the barracks where each of us received an army cot and blankets. Then we headed to a big mess hall for supper. There were lots and lots of displaced people there, just like us – poor. We were thankful for shelter and food; and stayed there three days. When we were settled in, we strolled up and down the compound and met a few people from our home town. Among them was Drescher Katibas, a very good friend of ours. A lot of stories were exchanged of our experience under the Partisans' cruel treatment. This was the first time we had seen her since we were all assembled on that dreadful night in our town square March 12, 1945. During the short time we were there, Dati had asked numerous people if they knew the direction to the border - crossing into Germany. One man told him to follow the river Salzach to Berchtesgaden; and when Dati had the directions, he immediately decided that we needed to move on the following day.

Dati told the man in charge of the Center that we had to move on and thanked him for all his help. When we left, a young, beautiful girl in her twenties from our hometown, Sentiwan, asked Dati if she could accompany us. Dati said, "Surely!" and she joined us. We walked a whole hour until we came to the border at Berchtesgaden, the place of entry into Germany.

The border guard came walking toward us and asked us, "Where are you going?"

Dati replied, "We want to go to Germany."

He asked us for our passports; and when Dati told him we didn't have any, he said, "Glaubt Ihr man kann ganz einfach nach Deutschland spazieren?" Translated, "Do you think one could simply just stroll into Germany?"

Dati explained to him what happened to our passports; but he wouldn't budge. He asked for the papers of the young lady that came with us. She also didn't have any; but she had money which she promised to give him if he let her cross. Therefore, he told her, "Go straight ahead." And he let her cross over. He would have accepted money from us; but we didn't have any, so he denied us. When Dati offered him a pack of cigarettes, he told us that he would let us cross; but not at the border crossing. He told us that we had to go over the mountain into Germany. He denied us the easy way; but he did take the pack of cigarettes and motioned for us to go up.

It was 11:00 a.m. when we started to climb uphill finally reaching the top at 8:00 p.m. It was a very steep mountain of brush and trees and some open patches of grass. We tried to pull us up holding on to branches and pushed up with our legs trying with all our might to make headway. Our leg muscles ached and burned and our arms were sore from pulling us upward. It was a constant struggle for nine hours.

When we came upon patches of grass, we lay down to rest and to catch our breath; and then moved on again. Several times when we dropped down, Mami kept saying, "I can't go on, I'm too exhausted, leave me alone, I can't go on. Then I would beg Mami, "please Mami, get up! You can't stay here all alone. We have to go on or it will be dark. I don't want to be here when it gets dark. Please, Mami try, please!"

I pulled her by the arms till she finally managed to pull herself together. When we finally reached the top, Mami almost could not walk, she was so exhausted. We were all dropping to the ground trying to recover. After a while, we lifted our heads, looking around. We were surprised to discover that the top of the mountain was flat; and that there was actually farmland up there. We saw a farmhouse and several cows and an electric tram wagon.

We lay there awhile, when our eyes caught a glimpse of a country woman walking toward us carrying a pitcher of milk in one hand and holding a glass in the other one. She came near and said, "Welcome to Berchtesgaden! Let me pour you a glass of milk - that should refresh you a bit." Then she poured each of us, one by one, a glass of milk. Boy! Did that ever taste good?

We thanked her from the bottom of our hearts. Then we realized what she had said when she said, "Welcome to Berchtesgaden!" Our faces lit up immediately; and we looked at each other with smiling faces. We realized all of a sudden that we had made it. We finally made it. This time it was true. "Praise God!" We finally made it – we were in Germany.

She went on to tell us that the tram would soon be leaving to the town of Berchtesgaden below; and that we could take it down free of charge. Hearing that, sounded like sweet music to our ears after having climbed up for nine hours. We rested a little while; and when she signaled that the tram was about to leave, we gathered up the knapsacks and headed for the tram, waving to her and yelling, "God bless you!" and thanking her again.

We boarded the tram and sat down and immediately were greeted with "Guten Abend!" Translated, "Good evening!" The greeting came from a Lutheran minister, already sitting. By looking at us, he knew we needed help and gave Dati $10 Mark.

When we reached bottom and got off the tram, he went and bought us train tickets to Bad Toelz for the next day and also paid for the ride to the Refugee Shelter nearby where we could stay for the night. We thanked him kindly; but there were no words sufficient to really express our gratitude – how thankful we really were. That night, sleeping in a bed again felt real good; and I was out like the light in no time.

In the morning, we washed up and after breakfast, headed for the railroad station. There were hundreds and hundreds of people waiting to board the train. There were no lines. Whoever got on first got the seats.

When it was time to go on board, there was such a commotion. Everyone was rushing and pushing, and rudely elbowing their way to make it aboard and not be left behind. As we saw people sitting and standing inside, filling the cars to their capacity and to start spilling out of the door and unto the platform, it seamed that we would not make it.

The conductor blew the whistle for the train to depart; and it slowly started to roll. All of a sudden Dati grabbed me and told Mami and Joschi to go for it. We ran with all our might and jumped up onto the running board, grabbed the handlebars and held on tightly. Just then the train set in full motion and the telephone poles systematically flew by. It seemed like they wanted to knock us off.

It was a very breezy ride. The distance was 100 Km (60 miles) from Berchtesgaden to Bad Toelz. It was hard to hold on all that way; but we dared not let go. Spotting a town in the distance eased my mind. I told myself, "Just hold on; it won't be long; we're almost there." When the train slowed down and finally came to a stop, we jumped off and rubbed our aching hands.

After we pulled ourselves together, Dati went to the information desk and asked for directions to the hospital where my cousin, Horn (surname) Karl, was employed. He was a skilled pottery maker. The hospital liked his work so much that they even built him a kiln so he could work at his trade right in the hospital. It was quite a long hike, but we found it. It was nice to see him again. He gave us directions to the Glockenhaus, a restaurant where Dati's sister, Horn Anna (called Noni-Bas) worked. The owner gave her room and board while she worked there. He told us to go there; and that he'd see us that night after work.

We went to the Glockenhaus and had no trouble spotting her. I was so happy to see her. I had not seen her since we were together in Gakowa. She was the one that cooked the sparrow for me that my brother, Joschi shot with a sling shot. Thanks be to God that we survived the death camp and were FREE, finally.

We stayed there a few days and she gave us a tour of the town after her work. Since we had entered Germany illegally and didn't have ID papers, Dati couldn't get a job anywhere in Bad Toelz, and that meant no food cards either. So we moved on.

Chapter 18
Settled In Munich

Our next stop was Munich at the Schneiders, my Dati's youngest sister, Rosi and Uncle Franz, and both my cousins Lisi and Franzi. We arrived in Munich in September of 1947; and temporarily stayed with them. They had escaped five months before we did; and they made it safely to Munich. When they arrived, they found housing in a former student dormitory of the bombed university on Ludwigs Strasse.

They let us move in with them for a while and shared their small living quarters and their food with us while Dati was trying to find a job. Their food card which provided for four persons now was stretched to feed eight.

One day in the afternoon I was so very hungry. My stomach yearned for a piece of bread. Mami and I were outside and I begged Mami "Mami please could I have just a little piece of bread?" I saw tears swelling up in Mami's eyes as she looked at me and said, "My dear child, I would give you some if I had some; but we don't have any food cards or money. Dati needs a job; and jobs are hard to come by with so many people looking for work. Rosl-Bas (Aunt Rosie) is already sharing their food with us; I can't ask her for more. You will have to wait till supper time."

There were piles and piles of rubble on the university property as a result of the bombings during World War II.

My cousins and I spent a lot of time digging in the rubble. There were all kinds of treasures to be found: spoons, forks, plates, etc. We enjoyed our stay there.

We were always close as a family; but Dati felt that he needed to get a job and support his family. It wasn't fair for them to give up their food for us too long, so we moved to the Refugee Center in Alach, outskirts of Munich. It offered shelter and food for the unemployed.

While we were there, we ran into the Fuderer family; and Hans-Vetter and the boys had a job remodeling bombed homes, with the Otto Kleibl Builders and Renovating Co. When Hans-Vetter found out that Dati did not have a job, he put in a good word for Dati and asked his employer the next day if they would hire him. When he came home after work, he came over to our barracks and told Dati that both Dati and Joschi could work there as their assistants.

There was a house located in the well-to-do area of Munich called Harlaching. The house belonging to Alis Weilinger had been damaged in a bombing raid. Hans-Vetter and his boys and Dati and Joschi were fixing it up and restoring it to its former beauty.

The only problem on our part was that the job was on the opposite side of Munich and Dati and my brother did not have the money for the cost of the street car fare back and forth on a daily basis.

On the first day they worked there, Dati noticed an auto garage in the rear to the left side of the house. It did not have a door because it blew out during a bombing.

A bright idea popped into Dati's mind. He asked the manager of the Co. for permission to fix up the garage and make it into temporary living quarters for him and his family till the repairs to her house was completed. That would take care of the problem of having to go back and forth. The manager told him he had to check with the owner of the house, Alice Weilinger, for an OK. She gave permission for us to move in there, till the repairs to her house were completed.

Dati got busy. He made a door from scrap lumber and installed it. Then he scrounged around for old bricks which he used to build an oven so that Mami could bake bread; and he made it so that it also would heat the garage at the same time since winter was approaching. Then he strung wire for electricity and when that was installed, we moved in Nov. 1, 1947. Our address was Munich 8, Harlaching, Arentinerstrasse 14.

Since we had a place to live and Dati's and Joschi's job was secured, Mami had a lot of running around to do to get us registered so that we could receive our own food cards.

First, she had to travel to a town called Freising to register us at the Refugee Employment Office. Then she made a trip to Allershausen to obtain the food ration cards, and last to Leonhartsbuch to register for housing.

A family received food cards once a month and one had to use the cards wisely. With the food cards, one could buy a certain amount of milk, bread, butter, eggs, flour, etc. and could only buy the amount shown on the card. If one ate up all the bread allowed the first week, then one had to do without till the next month.

When we moved into the auto garage, we received three Ami Betten (army cots) and ten pillows stuffed with straw and wool army blankets. One army cot served as a table. A board across the cot served as platform for our electric cooking ring. When we first moved in, we did not have any pots and pans. We had found a gallon size tin can which served as our cooking pot. Dati poked two holes opposite each other near the top of the can and strung a wire through, making a handle, so that Mami could carry it without getting burned. She cooked in it on our electric cooking ring; and when the meal was ended, it was washed out and used as a jug to get our daily milk ration. This "pot" had many uses.

Sometime later on, Joschi spotted a blue enamel pot in the rubble across the street where he worked; and to Mami's delight, she was so happy, she laid the gallon can to rest. She finally had a real cooking pot. We found our spoons, forks and knives by digging in the rubble. Those were our treasures.

Dati made a square frame from 2x4's and nailed it on top of each army cot and nailed a board over it big enough for two people to sleep on. One bed was against one wall of the garage and the other bed on the other side of the garage with our "table" in the middle. The cots also served as our chairs during the day.

Never would we have imagined three years prior that we would ever live in such poverty as we experienced at this time. After having lived in our own house with all the comforts of life; and Dati owning a very profitable business making wine barrels and wooden gear-driven washing machines for the whole town of Sentiwan and the surrounding area, it was hard to deal with.

Now we were poor, very poor. Mami called it "arm wie a Kerche Maus" poor like a church mouse; but we were thankful for what we had; and that our family was together.

Gakowa wiped out many a family. We had to make the best of what we had.

I remember one Christmas we spent together with the Schneiders. My cousin, Lisi, received a beautiful pair of ice skates that laced up. I secretly wished that I would have received ice skates like those; but we were too poor for such extravagant gifts. I don't remember what Franzi got; because I was so absorbed in those skates. Dati must have sensed my longing for skates in mine eyes, because a few days later, he presented me with skates that he had made of wood.

He had taken a 2X4 and cut it the length of my feet and tapered the sides so they looked like two wooden boats; and at the very bottom, he put a heavy wire like from a clothes hanger. Then he fashioned leather straps on the top side, so I could attach them to my boots and "sim-sala-bim!" I had skates made out of love. I could skate just as well as with expensive ones. I was sooo happy; I hugged him and hugged him. I put them on and looked for every frozen-over puddle I could find and skated across it. God is good!

Harlaching was a section of Munich where the well-to-do used to live. Now American soldiers and their families were housed there while they were stationed in Germany after the war. Therefore, American soldiers lived all around us. Our neighbor, an American soldier, had a butler; and he used to bring us a bag of charcoal briquettes every once in a while that would supplement our scrap wood which we used to heat with and make it burn through the night.

We lived there about a month, when one Saturday night we heard a knock on the door. Dati was not home from a remodeling job yet and it was already dark. Joschi went to open the door; and there in front of him stood an American soldier and a young lad. Joschi called Mami to the door while I slowly crept up, stood behind Mami and listened. The lad said, "My name is Chris and I was adopted by this American soldier. I used to be an orphan from the Russian Zone of Germany." The soldier was holding a Care package in his arms and he handed it over to Joschi and Chris translated what the American soldier told him to say.

He said, "This package is a gift from the Church of Christ located just around the corner at Lauderer Street, Nr.18. They have seen your poverty and want to help you." "We want to invite you to come and worship with us tomorrow at 10:00 a.m."

We said, "Danke Schoen!"

They both turned around and left while we, in bewilderment, slowly closed the door. We were so happy that we had received a gift; and we were wondering what could be inside; but we wanted to wait until Dati came home to open it. We could hardly wait.

When Dati walked in the door, I ran over to him and jumped up and down and said, "Look, look, what we've got, please hurry up and open it. Please hurry, please!" Dati opened it and he brought things out one by one of good things to eat. There was a box of Hershey's cocoa, flour, Domino sugar cubes, oatmeal, noodles, Crisco, Pet Milk, Cream of Wheat, cans of Spam, Wrigley's Chewing gum, macaroni, bars of Lux soap, and Hershey Chocolate bars. We hugged each other and cried; we were so happy. After enjoying a treat and saying a prayer of thanks, we turned in for the night.

Sunday morning, Dati told Mami that he would go to thank the people for the Care package. He set out to look for the church building. He went around the corner and walked up and down the street, checking the house numbers but could not find a church building.

After a while, the soldier and the young lad came toward him and told him that they are worshipping in the house and that Dati should go home and bring his family to worship with them.

Dati came back home and told Mami what they said. Mami looked at Dati and said, "I'm not going. Look at me. Look at my shoes - one shoe is bigger than the other one. What will people think?" Dati then said to Mami, "Come on let's just go anyway; they've been so nice to us." So we all went to the house.

They invited us into their beautiful furnished living room where a lot of folding chairs had been set up and everyone was already seated except the front row, those seats were empty.

Everyone was dressed so nice. Men wore soldier uniforms and the ladies wore pretty dresses and hats. We were dressed in rags. Everyone got up, introduced themselves shaking our hands and sincerely welcomed us into their midst. Then they seated us in the front row and sat back in their seats.

Everyone got real quiet for a moment and worship began. After a few joyous songs of praise in English and a prayer, and the passing around of the Lord's Supper, the preacher started his sermon, pausing at intervals, to give the translator a chance to interpret the words into German. We did not really hear all he said because we were just so embarrassed at the way we were dressed. We felt so out of place.

After worship was ended, we got up to leave, when Mrs. McDaniels came toward us with the lad to translate what she said and told us that Mami and I should come over to the house on Tuesday because they wanted to give us clothing to wear.

I could hardly wait till Tuesday. Well, Tuesday arrived and Mami and I walked over to them.

They welcomed us in and the lady took us upstairs into a room full of clothing. When she opened the door and I saw all kinds of pretty dresses, it seamed like I walked into heaven. Mami tried on clothes and I tried on clothes; and whatever we liked we could keep – coats, dresses, shoes, and everything in double. I was so happy. Mami was so happy. We finally looked like normal people. We kept saying "Danke Schoen, Danke Schoen, Danke Schoen" over and over; but there were no amount of words that we could have said to express our thanks.

They told us that on Saturday, Dati and Joschi should come over and pick out clothes for themselves also. We went home with armloads full of clothing. I could hardly wait for Dati and Joshi to come home from work so I could show them. They could not believe the amount of clothing we were given that day. I did not have to feel embarrassed anymore when I went out in public.

On Saturday, Dati and Joshi went and they also were outfitted with the clothes they needed, even clothes for work. We were reassured that God is good and He does provide for his children. One should never give up on God.

From then on we worshipped every Sunday with them in their house. We were also showered weekly with gifts of food all the while we were living in the garage. The soldier who had adopted Chris was Mr. Van Deusen; and the family in whose house worship was held was Mr. and Mrs. McDaniel. They had two young children – a girl about five years old and a boy about three years old.

I used to baby-sit for the McDaniels' when they went out. I enjoyed baby sitting at their house. They had real neat toys and beautiful dolls and doll furniture. Since I spent a good part of my childhood in the death camp, there were no toys there. I made my own dolls out of corn cobs. That was all there was.

Mrs. McDaniels often invited me to stay for supper after playing with their children. Their house was just around the corner a little ways from the auto garage.

I remember the first time I ate supper there. After a delicious meal, we had dessert. Mrs. McDaniel brought a tray with five glass goblets, each filled with red, strange looking jiggley squares piled on - one on top of another. As she walked, the squares jiggled back and forth; and there was a dollop of whipping cream on top. I wondered what that could be. I had never before seen anything like that.

She placed a goblet before me and gave me a spoon. I didn't know what to do with it; so I watched the children put it in their mouth. But when I tried to do the same and the spoon came close to my mouth, those little jiggley squares just slid right off my spoon and plopped back into my bowl and bounced around! It took me a while till I got the hang of it. It tasted like yummy raspberries, minus the berries. They must have been amused watching me eat Jello.

When spring arrived, the soldiers started to play baseball in the field a little distance from where we lived. We had never seen a game like that being played. The soldiers invited Dati and Joschi to play with them; and I, being curious, tagged along to see what it was all about. I didn't understand the game. I just noticed that the guys were running from pillow to pillow after hitting a ball with a prigl (bat).

After it was over, everyone shook hands and then food was passed around- a little long Wurst in a long cut open Semmel. They called it a hot dog. That was a strange name. Everyone also received a can of Coca Cola – I included. That ended my curiosity of the big flashing red Coca Cola sign on a building at night in Munich. I could not imagine what that sign stood for. I often wondered what Coca Cola represented. Now I knew. It tasted good and was cold. I was glad I tagged along and looked forward to the next game when I could also have a "hot dog" and a Coca Cola again. Spectators get hungry just as well as the ones that play the game.

As time went on, more and more German people came to worship at the McDaniels' house. Then in May 1948, a special missionary, brother, Otis Gatewood, who was the preacher in the church in Frankfurt, Germany, was invited to come and preach in German. My parents and brother plus six others responded to the invitation and were baptized by immersion in a river nearby.

Then Jack and Kay Nadeau and their three little girls, Deanna, Donna, and Janet came from the USA to Munich via Switzerland. Brother Nadeau was sent to be the preacher for the church in Munich. He secured a place where worship could be held since the Mc Daniel's house was getting overcrowded.

Jack and Kay had learned to speak the German language very well. We were very close. They became endeared in our hearts. We visited one another very frequently and spent many meals together. They gave us our first Bible.

Jack was a very powerful preacher. I learned a lot of Scriptures because of Jack and Kay's influence. They picked us up every week for worship and Bible study.

Shortly thereafter, several missionary couples moved to Munich.

There was Dick and Nell Smith who picked me up for Bible class even in the worst weather. They piled all the children they could into their small vehicle every week. They also invited us frequently for dinner after morning worship.

Dot Watson was responsible for my knowledge of the Book of Acts. She was a very good teacher. The Prochnows from Arkansas introduced me to my first taste of Macaroni and Cheese.

Then in the summer Jack Nadeau decided to have a tent meeting and invite everyone that would come to hear the gospel preached. A young missionary lady, Irene Johnson, came from Frankfurt to help with the door to door campaign of inviting people to the gospel meeting. My mother invited her to dinner one night, at which time Irene asked Mami if I could go along with her inviting people.

I was glad Mami gave her OK. Irene left a good impression on me from the moment I met her. I liked her enthusiasm.

The following day, Irene and I went knocking on doors. When people opened the door and asked what we wanted, Irene would invite them to come to the tent meeting to hear about God. When she mentioned God, we often got the door slammed into our face. Their reason was that God did not help them when they lost loved ones during the war and now they quit believing in Him.

When we had the door slammed in our face, Irene would always say, "I don't understand why people quit believing when they need God the most. She would always say, "Never give up on God!" And I wholeheartedly agreed with that statement. God does not remove trouble from our life; but if we trust Him and hold on, He will help us get through it. I can attest to that with all the bad experiences in my childhood. There is not a day that goes by that I don't think of Irene. She was a good influence in my life.

Nearly a year went by until the repair of the woodwork in Alis' house was completed and other repair crews took over. Otto Kleibl Co. had a new work assignment for Dati and Hans-Vetter and the boys. It was constructing wooden frames so that cement could be poured in between to make cement walls for a new chemical factory on the other side of town. While they were busy making the molds, Dati noticed barrels standing in the yard next to the new factory. Therefore, Dati decided to go on his lunch hour to inquire, if perhaps, they would be interested in hiring a barrel maker.

He went and asked the manager, Albert Bichler, if they needed help; and he in turn told Dati that he had to ask his boss and he would let him know his answer. He asked for Dati's address so that he could get in touch with him.

One evening a month later, Mr. Bichler came to see Dati at our home in the auto garage and told him that Mr. Ziegler would hire him if he was able to work on electric machinery. Mr. Ziegler did not have any employees that could work the electric machines. Dati told him that on the weekend he would come and demonstrate his knowledge of machinery and his skills as a barrel maker.

On Saturday Dati was off to see Mr. Ziegler. He examined the machines, none of them worked. They were dirty and highly neglected. Dati proceeded to clean them and oil all the necessary parts, and in no time had each machine running smoothly. He demonstrated his skills by cutting and planing the boards into shape. Mr. Ziegler was impressed and hired Dati immediately and made him manager of the company and paid him 70 DM a week.

He also employed Joschi, now 16 yrs. old, as a Fassbinder (barrelmaker) apprentice. That meant that Joschi had to go to school every morning for four years and when he came home from school, it was "hands on" learning to make barrels every afternoon. As an apprentice, Joschi received 5 DM a week. In 1948, it cost 3 DM to buy one loaf of bread; therefore, the salary for an apprentice wasn't all that much.

Joschi mastered the trade and made high quality barrels.

He even learned the art of carving. Dati and Mami were very proud of him and bought him a sharp looking bicycle with modern handlebars. He graduated in January, 1952 and received his Journey-man Degree. I was proud of my brother.

He was a handsome young man sitting on that bike. I used to shine his shoes for a quarter when he and his friend, Alex, who lived next door, went bike riding on the weekends. I saved up my quarters to buy a chocolate bar.

Mr. Ziegler also promised us living quarters at the firm. Mr. Ziegler's office was located in a large room as one walked past the machinery at the end of the workshop. Entering his office, to the left stood a stove, next was a table by a huge window with a view out into the yard -and then stood his desk. To the right everything was open with frames of 2x4 for storing the wood. Mr. Ziegler built a partition to the right and that became our living quarters.

We moved in November 1, 1948, and Mami took me to get registered to attend school for the first time since we were evacuated from our home. I was ten years old. I had never been to school before. Because of the war, the schools were closed in autumn of 1944 when I would have started first grade.

I was put in grade three because of my age, although I could not read or write or do math. It was a disaster. I could not get the hang of it. I was so embarrassed.

I was not in that grade too long when they demoted me. I was put in Grade two; and again I was s-o-o embarrassed because now I was a head taller than the rest of the class and was made fun of because of my ignorance. I finally got the hang of it and learned quickly and in the fall jumped two grades.

Classes started Monday –Friday 8:00 a.m. to noon and resumed 2:00 p.m. – 5:00 p.m. and on Saturday it was from 8:00 a.m. to noon.

Everyone owned a black slate board and a slate pencil. We did not use paper because it was just after the war and paper was very scarce. We only had one reading book.

Everything else we learned was copied onto our slate board; and we had to memorize it so that it could be erased from the slate board for our new assignments the following day. All of our math problems had to be memorized.

It took me one hour to walk to school and one hour back home. I lived the farthest from school than any of my school mates and there were no friends to play with. I enjoyed reading. Therefore, I thoroughly enjoyed reading from God's book. I came upon Psalms 23 one day and decided to memorize it; because it gave me comfort while walking home from school all alone in the dark in winter. Saying it over and over all the way home put away my fear.

Dati knew his profession very well and produced premium quality barrels. Mr. Ziegler was so pleased with Dati's work that he decided to enter Munich's Barrel maker Contest and won first prize in the city of Munich with the barrels Dati had made.

Mr. Ziegler was good to us. One day he brought us a radio so that we could have some entertainment and listen to music. One morning in 1951, Mami was listening to a radio program and during a break an announcement was made that refugees from Yugoslavia could apply to emigrate to the U.S.A. through the Christian Relief work Caritas. Mami went immediately to register.

It was the beginning of August in 1951. We had to fill out an application form, get a physical exam, X-rays and a lot of immunization shots, which was the worst part of it all. There was a lot of paperwork to be filled out. Everything seemed to go smoothly until one day we were notified that Dati's X-ray showed a scar on his lung and because of that, we could not go to America. They needed an explanation.

Dati told the doctor that he had pneumonia to the point of death in the concentration camp. The doctor gave him a thorough exam and then gave his OK.

What a relief! We were all looking forward to going to America. The Nadeaus had told us all about the U.S. and what a wonderful country it was and what a nice home we could make for ourselves. In Germany we were treated like refugees even though our ancestors had come from there. One had to work real hard and it was a constant struggle to make a go of it.

Food and clothing was scarce and very expensive. We could afford to buy only one egg at a time. When Mami used to send me to the store to buy an egg and I saw a bunch of bananas, I wished I could buy a banana to know what it tasted like; but we could not afford to buy even just one banana. Because eggs were so expensive, Mami had decided to raise some chickens; and soon thereafter, we had our own eggs. When the chickens were mature, Mami killed one occasionally and made fried chicken on Sundays. It pays if one learns to do things that helps one survive in bad times. Mami also knew how to raise our own vegetables.

After everything that was needed for the trip to America was taken care of, there came the long wait – waiting to see if we would be approved to go. One day we received the notification of our date of Departure – February 29, 1952. We were thrilled. Now it was time for us to eliminate things we could not take to America because we could only have one suitcase each. It was not a big problem because we did not own much.

One day Joschi came down with the mumps and because it is so contagious Mami wanted me to come down with it too so that we both would get over it and not miss our departure date. Despite Mami's efforts to get me exposed, I never came down with the mumps.

However, when Joschi reached the recovery stage, I woke up one morning, walked over to the wash basin to wash my face. Looking up into the mirror hanging above it, I noticed red spots all over my face. I panicked. I frantically called for Mami to examine me; and she confirmed what I had suspected – measles. She kept me home from school; and that was a good thing, because as the day progressed, I developed a real high fever.

We were all crushed because we knew that we had to postpone our trip. Mami had to go to the Funkkaserne to tell them about our predicament and hopefully be able to postpone our departure date. As I was recuperating in bed, I was upset with myself for getting sick. I could hardly wait for me to get better and loose my spots.

Another notification came for a new departure date – March 13 at the Bremen seaport. Mami packed our suitcases and the doctor was called to check me out to give his OK for me to travel. I was nervous for his answer because I could not go if I was still contagious. He checked me out and gave his OK, but admonished me to be very careful and make sure I wore a scarf and hat on the ship so that I wouldn't come down with a cold because my resistance was down.

We said good bye to our neighbors and Mr. Ziegler who was sad to loose his trusted employees. Then on February 29, 1952, we were off to the train station to buy a ticket to Bremen, the harbor where we would depart.

We joined the Schneiders who had also applied to go to America and we boarded the train together. Lisi, Franzi, and I were so excited. We had never before been on an ocean liner. We kept chattering with each other all the way there.

When we arrived in Bremen, we were put in special housing where we lived for thirteen days, waiting for the arrival of the ship from America. It was an exciting time. There were so many people gathered there, eagerly waiting to go to their new homeland.

I was wondering what America would be like when we got there. All things good that were scarce in Germany came from America. Dati had a cousin that lived in Detroit, Michigan. His name was Traub Toni Vetter. He provided housing for us when we got there and he also had found Dati a job as a barrel maker. Everything about our new homeland was going well. We had no worries about jobs and housing. Our missionary, Brother Jack Nadeau, even notified the Hayes Avenue Church of Christ in Detroit that we were on our way; and the congregation was waiting for our arrival. A nice couple, Mary and Chesley Quinn, had volunteered to pick us up for Sunday worship. God is good.

Photo Montage
Memories in Pictures

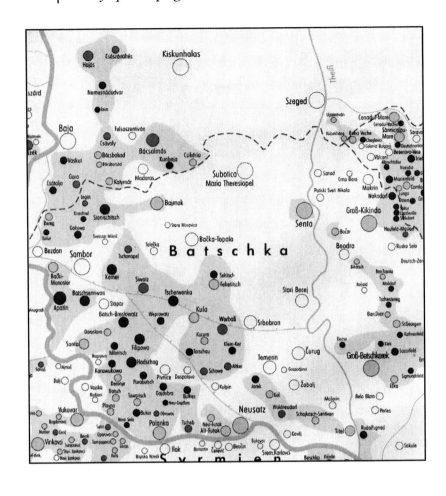

About the Author

Betty was born in Prigrevica Sveti Ivan, Yugoslavia an ethnic German. At the age of six, she and her entire town of the elderly and children were put into a Communist concentration camp for the annihilation of all ethnic Germans from 1945-1947. This was all carried out at the hand of Marshal Josip Broz Tito of Yugoslavia. His orders were all carried out at night while it was dark, so that the rest of the world did not know what he did.

She and her family escaped in May, 1947 into Hungary and traveled by foot until they reached Germany in September, 1947.

At the age of thirteen, Betty, along with her father, mother, and brother, immigrated to the U.S. in March, 1952 and settled in Detroit, MI. She took special English classes for three months. Webster's Dictionary was her constant companion. Betty attended Southeastern High School in Detroit, belonged to the National Honor Society, and graduated in 1956 with honors.

In 1958 Betty married George Spaltensperger. They have two children, Margaret and George, Jr., and three grand children.

After retirement, Betty and George moved up north and settled in the Gaylord, Michigan.

My memoirs were inspired by teachers and students from the Gaylord Middle School in Michigan. They urged me to write after hearing about my life in the concentration camp.